MILTON

Comus and other Poems

EDITED BY

F. T. PRINCE

D0824101

OXFORD UNIVERSITY PRESS

Oxford University Press, Great Clarendon Street, Oxford OX2 6DP

OXFORD NEW YORK
ATHENS AUCKLAND BANGKOK BOGOTÁ BUENOS AIRES
CALCUTTA CAPE TOWN CHENNAI DAR ES SALAAM
DELHI FLORENCE HONG KONG ISTANBUL KARACHI
KUALA LUMPUR MADRID MELBOURNE MEXICO CITY
MUMBAI NAIROBI PARIS SÃO PAULO SINGAPORE
TAIPEI TOKYO TORONTO WARSAW

and associated companies in
BERLIN IBADAN

Oxford is a trade mark of Oxford University Press

Introduction and Notes
© Oxford University Press 1968
Reprinted 1973, 1976 (twice), 1979, 1988, 1990, 1999

All rights reserved. No part of this publication may be
reproduced, stored in a retrieval system, or transmitted,
in any form or by any means, electronic, mechanical,
photocopying, recording, or otherwise, without the prior
permission of Oxford University Press.

Printed in China

CONTENTS

INTRODUCTION   v

NOTE ON THE TEXT   xvii

ON THE MORNING OF CHRIST'S
  NATIVITY   I

ON TIME   14

AT A SOLEMN MUSIC   15

L'ALLEGRO   17

IL PENSEROSO   23

ARCADES   30

COMUS   35

LYCIDAS   83

SONNETS   91

    I. To the Nightingale   91

    II. On His being Arrived to the Age of Twenty-Four 91

    III. When the Assault was Intended to the City 92

    IV. To a Virtuous Young Lady 93

    V. To the Lady Margaret Ley 94

    VI. On the Detraction which followed upon my
        Writing certain Treatises 95

    VII. On the Same 95

    VIII. To Mr. Henry Lawes, on His Airs 96

IX. On the Religious Memory of Mrs. Catharine Thomason, my Christian Friend, Deceased December, 1646   97

X. On the New Forcers of Conscience under the Long Parliament   98

XI. On the Lord General Fairfax, at the Siege of Colchester   99

XII. To the Lord General Cromwell, on the Proposals of certain Ministers at the Committee for Propagation of the Gospel, May 16, 1652   100

XIII. To Sir Henry Vane the Younger   100

XIV. On the late Massacre in Piemont   100

XV. On His Blindness   102

XVI. To Edward Lawrence   103

XVII. To Cyriack Skinner   103

XVIII. To the Same   104

XIX. On his deceased Wife   105

COMMENTARY   107

APPENDIX I. Renaissance Platonism and Cosmology   185

APPENDIX II. The Chronology of Milton's Life   195

INTRODUCTION

(i)

No English poet has played so great a part as Milton in a period of national crisis; the work of no other has been so shaped by the rise and fall of a revolutionary cause. His verse falls into two main divisions: the epic works of his later life, *Paradise Lost* (1667), and *Paradise Regain'd* with *Samson Agonistes* (1671); and the poems represented in this volume, which belong to his early and middle years. The division is marked by the Restoration of the monarchy in 1660; as the nation rejected the Puritan Commonwealth, Milton turned back to his plans for religious epic, which he had been forced to postpone for so long.

The poetry written before *Paradise Lost* also falls into two phases which reflect the course of events: the first ends with *Lycidas* in 1637, the second gives us most of the Sonnets. The two phases are separated by Milton's journey to Italy (1638–9). The verse of the previous ten years represents his education as a poet, the dedicated studies of a young man who is not yet ready to launch out into active life. But when Milton returned from abroad, the struggle between King and Parliament was about to begin. The next twenty years were full of political and religious strife, in which Milton gave all he had to give, and sacrificed finally his sight. His public life, together with his experience of love and marriage, can be described as Milton's education as a man.

(ii)

Poetry, music, and religion were the three intellectual passions of Milton's life; for him the two arts, and faith and moral integrity, seem to have been so closely linked that they lived and grew as one. The vision of Heaven's glory which recurs throughout his verse is always translated into images of music and song; he celebrates the beauty of the created universe, and the achievement of virtue by man, in terms of measure and harmony. His love of beauty extends to the love of goodness as a form of beauty. Through poetry, music, and traditional religious ideas, he can express what he sees and feels; and they provide him not only with the means of expression, but with images of final truth.

The ways in which Milton's threefold passion guided him can be traced most clearly in the work of his youth. There almost every poem is a step in self-discovery; and he discovers himself by exploring what music, poetry, and religion mean to him, and where they take him. Above all, in practice the link between them is not only the idea of divine inspiration which is the basis of Christian Platonism: it is made also by Milton's own experience, apparent in his poetry from first to last, that 'inspiration' was a decisive reality for him.

(iii)

When we say that Milton is a learned poet, we should also point out the direct relationship between his learning and his inspiration. As he has told us, he first revealed himself as a poet in the course of his education. When he was a boy, in his exercises in Latin and English composition, and chiefly in those in verse, 'it was found that . . . the style, by certain vital signs it had, was likely to live'.[1] This early experience may have determined his life-long habit of

[1] *The Reason of Church-Government*, 1642 (from which subsequent quotations in this section are also taken).

setting himself to fulfil the demands of a given form; he could hope that, as he worked, his enthusiasm would be kindled and inspiration would come.

In 1629, at the age of twenty-one, the apprentice to poetry wrote his first masterly poem, the Nativity Ode. From then on his life had a fixed purpose, so ambitious that it laid itself open to many doubts and disappointments: 'that by labour and intent study (which I take to be my portion in this life) joined with the strong propensity of nature, I might perhaps leave something so written to after-times, as they should not willingly let it die'.

'Intent study' was indeed always to be the frame and support of Milton's poetic vision, and as much his vocation as the art of poetry. Even at twenty-one he could look back on ten years or more of hard work. His father, who had prospered in business, was deeply religious, a lover of learning, and an accomplished amateur musician; and he fostered the gifts which his son showed in childhood, providing him with private tutors both before and after he went to school. Thus at St. Paul's, and later at Cambridge, Milton only added a traditional education shared by others, to the special formation he had been given at home (for example, in music and in Italian). His father gave the first direction to his interests, and also the money needed for a prolonged education. Milton remained ever conscious of a great debt, not least when he decided that he should persist in study for a longer period than his father could have foreseen. It may have been a disappointment to the elder Milton when his son did not enter the Church, for at one time that had been intended. Milton attributed his drawing back from ordination to the policies of Laud; but poetry may have called him irresistibly, and he could add the argument that it might be a powerful instrument of his religious convictions.

Milton shaped for himself the later stages of his education. After completing seven years at Cambridge in 1632, he entered on five years of private study at Horton, near Windsor, where his father had a small house. Having decided on this course, Milton disarmed his father's criticisms, in Latin verses defending his dedication to poetry. He argues that his father, as a musician, should acknowledge that music is incomplete without song, the articulate thought of the poet; music and poetry are twins, and the divinest of human arts. So Milton was given yet more 'ease and leisure' for study, 'out of the sweat of other men'.

Milton's programme of study at Horton was planned generously, as the equipment of a future epic poet. Much of the historical, theological, and classical learning he acquired was to be used, not only in the later poetry, but in the intervening period of political debate and action. But we need not imagine Milton living at Horton only as a scholarly recluse. London was near, and there he had spent and was to spend the greater part of his life. Oxford was not far away, and he did not lose touch with friends at Cambridge. The performance of *Comus* at Ludlow must have entailed a journey to the Welsh border, and Milton may have ranged further, in view of his interest in British antiquities. *Arcades* and *Comus* brought him an acquaintance with one of the great families at Court. His intelligence and good looks, his literary talent, and his idealism would recommend him in any society that was likely to please him. The letter Sir Henry Wotton wrote, after the gift of a copy of *Comus*, shows that this young new acquaintance, and his poems, had much impressed the old diplomatist.

The atmosphere of his life at Horton is distilled into the poetry, and especially into *L'Allegro* and *Il Penseroso*. He lets his imagination play over Renaissance philosophy, mythology, English poetry, and music; and sees the pleasures of the Court and of town-life as part of the dream-like pageant. Study in solitude brings the excitement of pursuing hidden doctrines, and an apprehension of supernatural light shining through Nature and art. He relishes the homely sweetness of country life, and the round of seasonal work on the land; but he writes almost always as a spectator.

Milton had a poet's capacity for happiness; but his poetic vision was always bought at a price. The price was thought and labour, a conscious withdrawal from common life, and recurrent anxieties. A man who believes that he is potentially an inspired poet, and that he is called upon to use the gift well, can expect no easy path in life. Even if we do not share Milton's idea of vocation, we can see that poetic genius carries with it peculiar fears, which correspond with its peculiar rewards. A pattern of strain and trial can be traced in Milton's verse from beginning to end. His last great poem, *Samson Agonistes*, is wrought out of pain, doubt, a sense of betrayal and defeat, leading to certainty and tragic triumph—it enacts the failure of inspiration, and its unpredictable return. In his early twenties, encouraged by the success of the Nativity Ode, he attempts a poem on the Passion, finds that inspiration will not come, and leaves it unfinished. The sonnet *To the Nightingale* pleads rather diffidently for good fortune, not only in love, but in poetry; that on his 24th birthday broods over the slow progress he is making. The poems of the Horton period alone convey a mood of liberation and growing confidence. But a year or two later, in *Lycidas*, a young

friend's death plunges him into radical questioning, with a
revulsion from the 'uncessant care' of 'the homely slighted
shepherd's trade', and 'the thankless Muse'.

It is true that all those poems in which we can follow
Milton's quarrel with himself or with God, end with a
recovery of faith, and with the acceptance of his task. But
the struggle is not the less real for its victorious outcome.
Milton may be inspired by debate, it may bring him his
greatest rewards, in life as in art; but none of this could
happen if the conflict did not lie deep in his nature.

(iv)

The Italian journey (1638–9) separated Milton's youth
from his middle life, and was the fitting crown of his
poetic education. His classical studies had to be completed
by a visit to Rome and Naples, and to be measured against
the standards of Italian scholars. The supreme object of his
ambition was to write an English epic, and Tasso's *Jerusalem
Delivered* was admired as the greatest Christian example of
the kind. Milton was to find in Italy the key to his creation
of an English epic style in *Paradise Lost*.

Milton stayed first in Florence, which had seen the birth
of Italian literature three centuries before, and was still the
literary centre. There he made lasting friends among men
of letters, who admired his Latin compositions and his
personal qualities. After two months he went on to
Rome, where his outspoken hostility to the Church did not
prevent his being appreciated and kindly entertained; and
to Naples, where he met Tasso's former patron, Manso.
News then reached him from England, of the dispute
between the King and the Scottish Covenanters, and he
decided that he could not remain abroad when such important matters were likely to be settled at home. But he took

time over the return journey, spending again two months in
Rome and two in Florence, and visiting Venice; he arrived
back in England in the late summer of 1639.

(v)

Soon after returning from abroad, Milton rented a house
in London, in Aldersgate Street. The city had been his
home, and it was the natural centre for an independent man
of genius, a 'free and splendid wit'. Presumably Milton
also wished to be on the scene where national issues were
decided. But at first he only resumed his scholarly life,
taking some private pupils and finding time to weigh themes
for heroic poetry and drama.[1] In 1640 the King's military
and political weakness was exposed by the Second Bishops'
War, and he had to summon a Parliament in November.
The Long Parliament (as it was to be) was strongly Puritan;
it established freedom of speech, and set going the debate
on religion and political liberty which was to continue for
twenty years.

When those years ended Milton was over fifty, and had
had experience of the life of action and of many personal
vicissitudes. There could hardly be a greater contrast than
that between this period and his early life, when he had
been free from practical problems and dedicated to his art
and secluded study. The contrast is illustrated by the verse
written in the two periods. The Latin and English poems
of his youth are in various forms, suggesting that they are
chosen for exercise or experiment; they heap up rich
language and imagery, and have been built up at leisure on
a basis of careful thought. The poems of the middle years,

---

[1] A manuscript in possession of Trinity College, Cambridge, contains,
in addition to versions of many of the minor poems, a list of possible
subjects for tragedies, drawn up after Milton's return from Italy.

the Sonnets, repeat one form which he has already mastered, and their language is generally compressed and bare; some of them are written under the spur of immediate emotion, some in reflective intervals between other tasks. They are direct personal utterances, while the earlier poems are often dramatic in form, or otherwise 'distanced' from the poet's daily life.

In their echoes of current events, their references to controversy, and their addresses to soldiers and statesmen of the Commonwealth, the Sonnets clearly point to Milton's chief activities of that time. Yet even in becoming a public figure and a partisan, he was anxious to declare himself first and foremost a poet, as he does in the first Sonnet (III) of the Civil War period. So, in his first pamphlet on religious reform, he looks forward to an early settlement that may bring him fulfilment as a poet: 'Then amidst the Hymns and Hallelujahs of Saints someone may perhaps be heard offering at high strains in new and lofty measures, to sing and celebrate God's divine mercies and marvellous judgements in this land throughout all ages. . . .' When he was attacked for coming forward as a controversialist, he tried to explain why he felt forced to do so, though he was by nature and ambition a poet.[1] When he collected and published his verse in 1645, it was to give substance to the claim.

Yet everything that happened carried him steadily further away from poetry. The divisions of opinion in the country proved to be irreconcilable, and one Civil War was followed by another. Even the victories of Cromwell's New Model Army brought a settlement no nearer. Soon after Milton had completed his first batch of controversial writings, he married, and was presented with new and

[1] In *The Reason of Church-Government.*

disturbing problems. These set him off on a new round of prose controversy, and might in any case have been an obstacle to free poetic creation.

In the summer of 1642 Milton married Mary Powell, the daughter of a country gentleman living near Oxford; she was a girl of seventeen, and did not care for the quiet life Milton offered her in London, 'after having been used to a great house and much company and joviality' (Edward Phillips). After only a few weeks of marriage, she was invited back to her family for a visit, and stayed longer than Milton had expected; he was forced to realize that she was reluctant to return. The varying course of the Civil War had a bearing on their relationship. The King's headquarters were at Oxford, and the Powells were Royalists. When the King's Army won its first victory at Edgehill in October 1642, Mary Powell may have felt justified in remaining with her parents, rather than rejoining a husband on what appeared to be the losing side. It was not until after the decisive defeat of the Royalists by Cromwell at Naseby, in 1645, that Mrs. Milton went to London and was reconciled to her husband. When Oxford fell to the Parliamentary forces a year later, the Powell family took refuge in Milton's London house, having lost their means of support.

The series of divorce tracts began about a year after Mary Powell left Milton. In them he argues that marriage should be a union of minds and hearts as well as of bodies, and that this ideal cannot be followed unless divorce is granted in cases where the partners have not achieved it. Milton maintained that his plea for greater freedom of divorce was a logical extension of the political and religious freedom which he had already upheld, and for which half the nation was fighting. Yet we cannot miss the note of personal bitterness in his arguments, or doubt that the problem had been forced on his attention by his own disappointing experience. However, we must not forget that it was a case of disappointed love, and that he forgave his wife when she appealed to him; they lived together for seven years, and she bore him four children.

The effect of Milton's first marriage on his poetic vision can be estimated if at all—only by considering the great poems of his later life. The immediate consequence of his unhappiness was the divorce tracts; and the consequence of these was his break with the Presbyterians, whom he had supported in their campaign against episcopacy. He now rejected their policy of uniformity in religion, and their wish to suppress freedom of speech. *Areopagitica* (1644), the finest of his prose works, was an attack on the proposal in Parliament for a new censorship of all printed matter. From then on, Milton in the Sonnets refers to the danger of a new ecclesiastical tyranny, if anything worse than that of the Laudian Church (VII, X, XII); and he allied himself with the Independents in Parliament, who were led by Cromwell and backed by the Army. The trial and execution of the King led him to defend Cromwell's policy against adverse opinion both at home and in Europe: thus he wrote the two massive *Defences of the English People* (1651, 1654) in Latin, in order to reach an international public.

Milton so became the chief spokesman, in print, of Cromwell's government, and it was not long before the burden of work he had undertaken cost him his sight. His eyes were weak, and had begun to fail some years earlier; his blindness became total in 1652, and his official work had first to be reduced, and finally taken over by others. The later Sonnets give us the Milton who was to be free to turn back to the long-deferred task of poetry: the blind seer who has lost his sight in defence of his country's liberty (XV, XVIII), but who has never ceased to think of an epic poem as the true purpose of his life.

(vi)

One event of overwhelming importance to Milton was yet to come: the abandonment of the Puritan Commonwealth by the English people, and their return to monarchy and a Church Establishment. Milton's convictions were strengthened rather than weakened by this change in national opinion, and he persisted to the end in the attempt to avert the betrayal of all he had fought for. To the practical difficulties entailed by his blindness were now added the experience of personal danger, loss of property and income, and an obscure way of life under a new system he detested. Yet it was in these circumstances that *Paradise Lost* was composed, and published in 1667.

All poetry is born of life, both the life of the poet and the life of his time. The poems Milton wrote before his great epics have an especial value as evidence of his long and slow development in youth, and of the action and suffering of his middle years; but the best of them are also transcendent works of art, with a powerful and radiant life of their own.

NOTE ON THE TEXT

MOST of the poems in this volume were published by Milton himself, in the collection of *Poems by Mr. John Milton, both English and Latin, Compos'd at several times*, which he brought out first in 1645, and again, revised and enlarged, in 1673. Only the first five Sonnets were included in the first edition; ten others were added in the second, but four (XI, XII, XIII, XVIII) did not appear until they were printed by Milton's nephew Edward Phillips in 1694. For the latter we have also the authority of the manuscript at Trinity College, Cambridge, which contains versions of many of the minor poems, most of them in Milton's autograph.

The original spelling, punctuation, and capitalization have been normalized, with the object of removing as many difficulties as possible.

On the Morning of Christ's Nativity

COMPOSED 1629

I

THIS is the month, and this the happy morn
Wherein the Son of Heaven's eternal King,
Of wedded Maid and Virgin Mother born,
Our great redemption from above did bring;
For so the holy sages once did sing,
  That he our deadly forfeit should release
And with his Father work us a perpetual peace.

II

That glorious form, that light unsufferable,
And that far-beaming blaze of majesty,
Wherewith he wont at Heaven's high council-table 10
To sit the midst of Trinal Unity,
He laid aside; and here with us to be,
  Forsook the courts of everlasting day
And chose with us a darksome house of mortal clay.

III

Say, Heavenly Muse, shall not thy sacred vein
Afford a present to the Infant God?
Hast thou no verse, no hymn or solemn strain,

---

6 *deadly forfeit*: the punishment of death incurred by the Fall of Man.
'Forfeit' meant 'misdeed', but acquired the meaning of 'penalty'.   7 'And
bring about a perpetual peace between us and God the Father.'   8 *unsufferable*: unbearable.   10 *wont*: was accustomed.   11 *Trinal*:
threefold.   15 *vein*: talent or style.   17 *strain*: piece of music.
Cf. *L'Allegro*, l. 148, *Comus*, ll. 494, 561, etc.

To welcome him to this his new abode,
Now while the heaven, by the sun's team untrod,
   Hath took no print of the approaching light,   20
And all the spangled host keep watch in squadrons bright?

IV

See how from far upon the eastern road
The star-led Wizards haste with odours sweet!
O run, prevent them with thy humble ode,
And lay it lowly at his blessèd feet;
Have thou the honour first thy Lord to greet,
   And join thy voice unto the angel quire,
From out his secret altar touch'd with hallow'd fire.

20 *print*: impression.   23 *Wizards*: magicians, Magi.   24 *prevent them*: forestall them.

The Hymn

I

IT was the winter wild,
While the Heaven-born child   30
  All meanly wrapp'd in the rude manger lies;
Nature in awe to him
Had doff'd her gaudy trim,
  With her great Master so to sympathize:
It was no season then for her
To wanton with the sun, her lusty paramour.

II

Only with speeches fair
She woos the gentle air
  To hide her guilty front with innocent snow,
And on her naked shame,   40
Pollute with sinful blame,
  The saintly veil of maiden white to throw—
Confounded, that her Maker's eyes
Should look so near upon her foul deformities.

III

But he, her fears to cease,
Sent down the meek-eyed Peace;

30 *While*: at that time when.   31 *rude*: simple.   33 *doff'd her gaudy trim*: 'taken off her gay clothing', i.e. leaves and flowers.   36 *wanton*: play. *paramour*: lover.   41 *Pollute*: polluted, stained.   43 *Confounded*: dismayed.   45 *cease*: make cease.

She, crown'd with olive green, came softly sliding
Down through the turning sphere,
His ready harbinger,
    With turtle wing the amorous clouds dividing;   50
And waving wide her myrtle wand,
She strikes a universal peace through sea and land.

IV

No war or battle's sound
Was heard the world around,
    The idle spear and shield were high up-hung;
The hookèd chariot stood
Unstain'd with hostile blood,
    The trumpet spake not to the armèd throng;
And kings sate still with awful eye,
As if they surely knew their sovran Lord was by.   60

V

But peaceful was the night
Wherein the Prince of Light
    His reign of peace upon the earth began:
The winds with wonder whist
Smoothly the waters kiss'd,
    Whispering new joys to the mild ocean,
Who now hath quite forgot to rave,
While birds of calm sit brooding on the charmèd wave.

    49 *harbinger*: forerunner, messenger sent in advance.   50 *turtle wing*:
the wings of the turtle dove.   *amorous*: loving (towards Peace).
56 *hookèd*: fitted with hooks (on the wheels).   59 *awful*: filled with
awe.   60 *sovran*: Milton's usual spelling of 'sovereign' (Ital. *sovrano*).
64 *whist*: hushed. Cf. *The Tempest*, I. ii: 'The wild waves whist.'
66 *ocean*: pronounce 'o-ce-an'.   68 *charmèd*: spell-bound.

VI

The stars with deep amaze
Stand fix'd in steadfast gaze,   70
   Bending one way their precious influence,
And will not take their flight,
For all the morning light
   Or Lucifer that often warn'd them thence;
But in their glimmering orbs did glow
Until their Lord himself bespake, and bid them go.

VII

And though the shady gloom
Had given day her room,
   The sun himself withheld his wonted speed,
And hid his head for shame,   80
As his inferior flame
   The new-enlighten'd world no more should need:
He saw a greater Sun appear
Than his bright throne or burning axle-tree could bear.

VIII

The shepherds on the lawn,
Or ere the point of dawn,
   Sate simply chatting in a rustic row;
Full little thought they than,
That the mighty Pan
   Was kindly come to live with them below.   90

71 *one way*: in one direction only.   *influence*: inflowing power. Cf.
L'Allegro, l. 122, *Comus*, l. 336, etc.   75 *orbs*: orbits.   76 *bespake*:
spoke out. Cf. *Lycidas*, l. 112.   78 *given day her room*: made way for day.
81 *As*: as if.   84 *axle-tree*: the pole forming the axle of the sun's
chariot. Cf. *Lycidas*, l. 25.   85 *lawn*: grassy plain.   86 *Or ere*:
before.   88 *than*: then.   90 *kindly*: familiarly.

Perhaps their loves, or else their sheep,
Was all that did their silly thoughts so busy keep:

IX

When such music sweet
Their hearts and ears did greet,
    As never was by mortal finger strook—
Divinely-warbled voice
Answering the stringèd noise,
    As all their souls in blissful rapture took;
The air, such pleasure loth to lose,
With thousand echoes still prolongs each heavenly
        close.   100

X

Nature that heard such sound
Beneath the hollow round
    Of Cynthia's seat, the airy region thrilling,
Now was almost won
To think her part was done,
    And that her reign had here its last fulfilling:
She knew such harmony alone
Could hold all Heaven and Earth in happier union.

XI

At last surrounds their sight
A globe of circular light   110

92 *silly*: simple, innocent.   95 *strook*: struck.   96 *warbled*: modulated in song.   97 *noise*: music, or band of instruments.   99 *loth*: unwilling.   100 *close*: cadence in music.   103 *thrilling*: piercing.
104 *won*: persuaded.

That with long beams the shame-faced night array'd;
The helmèd Cherubim
And sworded Seraphim
  Are seen in glittering ranks with wings display'd,
Harping in loud and solemn quire
With unexpressive notes to Heaven's new-born Heir.

XII

Such music (as 'tis said)
Before was never made
  But when of old the Sons of Morning sung,
While the Creator great   120
His constellations set,
  And the well-balanced world on hinges hung,
And cast the dark foundations deep,
And bid the weltering waves their oozy channel keep.

XIII

Ring out, ye crystal spheres,
Once bless our human ears
  (If ye have power to touch our senses so),
And let your silver chime
Move in melodious time,
  And let the bass of heaven's deep organ blow,   130
And with your ninefold harmony
Make up full consort to th'angelic symphony.

111 *shame-faced*: hiding or covering its face.   115 *Harping*:
playing harps.   116 *unexpressive*: inexpressible. Cf. *Lycidas*, l. 176.
122 *hinges*: the two poles making the earth's axis.   124 *weltering*:
rolling. Cf. *Lycidas*, l. 13.   126 *Once*: only.   128 *chime*: concord. Cf. *At a Solemn Music*, l. 20.   132 *consort*: harmony.

XIV

For if such holy song
Enwrap our fancy long,
   Time will run back and fetch the age of gold,
And speckled Vanity
Will sicken soon and die,
   And leprous Sin will melt from earthly mould,
And Hell itself will pass away
And leave her dolorous mansions to the peering day.   140

XV

Yea, Truth and Justice then
Will down return to men,
   Orb'd in a rainbow; and, like glories wearing,
Mercy will sit between
Throned in celestial sheen,
   With radiant feet the tissued clouds down steering;
And Heaven, as at some festival,
Will open wide the gates of her high palace hall.

XVI

But wisest Fate says No,
This must not yet be so;   150
   The Babe lies yet in smiling infancy,
That on the bitter cross
Must redeem our loss,
   So both himself and us to glorify.

134 *Enwrap*: engross, enrapture. Cf. l. 98.   *fancy*: cf. *At a Solemn Music*,
l. 5.   136 *speckled*: spotted (with sin).   138 *mould*: clay (of which
man is made). Cf. *Comus*, l. 17.   140 *dolorous*: full of pain.   *mansions*:
dwelling-places, or compartments.   143 *Orb'd in*: encircled by.
like: similar.   145 *sheen*: brightness.   146 *tissued*: woven.
steering: directing her course.

Yet first to those ychain'd in sleep
The wakeful trump of doom must thunder through the
    deep,

XVII

With such a horrid clang
As on Mount Sinai rang
    While the red fire and smouldering clouds out-brake:
The agèd Earth aghast   160
With terror of that blast
    Shall from the surface to the centre shake,
When at the world's last session
The dreadful Judge in middle air shall spread his throne.

XVIII

And then at last our bliss
Full and perfect is,
    But now begins; for from this happy day
Th'old Dragon under ground,
In straiter limits bound,
    Not half so far casts his usurpèd sway,   170
And wroth to see his kingdom fail,
Swinges the scaly horror of his folded tail.

155 *ychain'd*: chained up; *y-* represents the Old English *ge-*, the prefix
to the past participle.   156 *wakeful*: rousing.   *doom*: judgement.
163 *session*: pronounce 'sessi-on'.   166 *is*: The present tense is used
for the future, giving an effect of vividness, and also conveying that the
Last Judgement is outside time, like the Nativity, which 'now begins'
(l. 167).   169 *straiter*: narrower.   170 *casts his usurpèd sway*: extends
the power he has usurped.   172 *Swinges*: 'A form of "swing" that
retained the senses of "flog" and "brandish", and so was used of a beast
"lashing" its tail' (Wright).   *horror*: Milton often uses an abstract noun
to describe something concrete, giving an effect of indefinite, mysterious
power.

XIX

The oracles are dumb:
No voice or hideous hum
  Runs through the archèd roof in words deceiving;
Apollo from his shrine
Can no more divine,
  With hollow shriek the steep of Delphos leaving;
No nightly trance or breathèd spell
Inspires the pale-eyed priest from the prophetic cell.   180

XX

The lonely mountains o'er
And the resounding shore
  A voice of weeping heard and loud lament;
From haunted spring and dale
Edged with poplar pale,
  The parting Genius is with sighing sent;
With flower-inwoven tresses torn
The nymphs in twilight shade of tangled thickets mourn.

XXI

In consecrated earth
And on the holy hearth   190
  The Lars and Lemures moan with midnight plaint;
In urns and altars round
A drear and dying sound
  Affrights the Flamens at their service quaint;

174 *hideous*: frightening.   179 *nightly*: nocturnal.   182 *re-sounding*: i.e. with the breaking or lapping of water.   194 *service quaint*: ingenious or elaborate ritual. Cf. *Arcades*, l. 47, *Comus*, l. 157 and *Lycidas*, l. 139. 'Quaint' originally meant 'skilful', and referred to something done or made with care; hence it came to mean 'fine, curious', or 'fantastic', and now merely 'odd'.

And the chill marble seems to sweat,
While each peculiar power forgoes his wonted seat.

XXII

Peor and Baälim
Forsake their temples dim,
  With that twice-batter'd god of Palestine;
And moonèd Ashtaroth,   200
Heaven's queen and mother both,
  Now sits not girt with tapers' holy shine;
The Libyc Hammon shrinks his horn;
In vain the Tyrian maids their wounded Thammuz mourn.

XXIII

And sullen Moloch, fled,
Hath left in shadows dread
  His burning idol all of blackest hue;
In vain with cymbals' ring
They call the grisly king,
  In dismal dance about the furnace blue.   210
The brutish gods of Nile as fast,
Isis and Orus and the dog Anubis, haste.

XXIV

Nor is Osiris seen
In Memphian grove or green,
  Trampling the unshower'd grass with lowings loud;
Nor can he be at rest
Within his sacred chest:
  Naught but profoundest Hell can be his shroud.

196 *peculiar power*: particular spirit or god. *forgoes*: deserts. *seat*:
dwelling-place, temple.   202 *girt*: surrounded. *shine*: brightness.
203 *shrinks*: draws in; transitive, as in *Lycidas*, l. 133.   218 *shroud*:
covering.

In vain with timbrell'd anthems dark
The sable-stolèd sorcerers bear his worshipp'd ark: 220

XXV

He feels from Juda's land
The dreaded Infant's hand;
　The rays of Bethlehem blind his dusky eyne.
Nor all the gods beside
Longer dare abide,
　Not Typhon huge ending in snaky twine:
Our Babe, to show his Godhead true,
Can in his swaddling bands control the damnèd crew.

XXVI

So, when the sun in bed,
Curtain'd in cloudy red,   230
　Pillows his chin upon an orient wave,
The flocking shadows pale
Troop to the infernal jail;
　Each fetter'd ghost slips to his several grave,
And the yellow-skirted fays
Fly after the night-steeds, leaving their moon-loved maze.

XXVII

But see, the Virgin blest
Hath laid her Babe to rest:

219 *timbrell'd*: accompanied by timbrels (i.e. small drums or tambourines).　　220 *sable-stolèd*: black-robed.　　223 *dusky eyne*: dark eyes. 'Eyne' as the plural of 'eye' was passing out of use in Milton's time. 225 *snaky twine*: a serpent's twisting tail.　　228 *crew*: company. Cf. *L'Allegro*. l. 38.　　231 *orient*: eastern.　　233 *the infernal jail*: Hell their prison.　　234 *several*: separate.

Time is our tedious song should here have ending.
Heaven's youngest-teemèd star   240
Hath fix'd her polish'd car,
    Her sleeping Lord with handmaid lamp attending;
And all about the courtly stable
Bright-harness'd angels sit in order serviceable.

---

240 *youngest-teemèd*: latest born. Cf. *Comus*, l. 175.   244 *Bright-harness'd*: in bright armour.   *serviceable*: ready for service.

On Time

FLY, envious Time, till thou run out thy race,
Call on the lazy leaden-stepping hours
Whose speed is but the heavy plummet's pace;
And glut thyself with what thy womb devours,
Which is no more than what is false and vain
And merely mortal dross:
So little is our loss,
So little is thy gain.
For whenas each thing bad thou hast entomb'd,
And last of all, thy greedy self consumed,   10
Then long Eternity shall greet our bliss
With an individual kiss;
And Joy shall overtake us as a flood,
When everything that is sincerely good
And perfectly divine,
With Truth and Peace and Love shall ever shine
About the supreme throne
Of Him, t'whose happy-making sight alone
When once our heavenly-guided soul shall climb,
Then all this earthy grossness quit,   20
Attired with stars, we shall forever sit,
Triumphing over Death, and Chance, and thee, O Time.

1 *envious*: malicious.   3 *the heavy plummet's pace*: the slow swing of
the lead pendulum (of the clock on whose case the poem is to be inscribed).   4 *glut*: fill.   *womb*: belly.   6 *dross*: impure matter.
9 *whenas*: when.   12 *individual*: not to be divided, indissoluble.
14 *sincerely*: purely.   17 *supreme*: accent on the first syllable.
18 *happy-making sight*: 'the plain English of *beatific vision*, the vision of
God granted to the saints after death' (Wright).   20 *quit*: quitted, left
off.   21 *Attired*: crowned.

At a Solemn Music

BLEST pair of Sirens, pledges of Heaven's joy,
Sphere-born harmonious sisters, Voice and Verse,
Wed your divine sounds, and mix'd power employ,
Dead things with inbreathed sense able to pierce;
And to our high-raised phantasy present
That undisturbèd song of pure concent,
Aye sung before the sapphire-colour'd throne
To him that sits thereon,
With saintly shout and solemn jubilee,
Where the bright Seraphim in burning row   10
Their loud uplifted angel-trumpets blow,
And the Cherubic host in thousand quires
Touch their immortal harps of golden wires,
With those just spirits that wear victorious palms,
Hymns devout and holy psalms
Singing everlastingly:
That we on Earth with undiscording voice
May rightly answer that melodious noise;
As once we did, till disproportion'd sin
Jarr'd against Nature's chime, and with harsh din   20
Broke the fair music that all creatures made
To their great Lord, whose love their motion sway'd

1 *pledges*: children; the sense includes that of 'tokens, promises'. Cf.
Lycidas, l. 107.   2 *sphere-born*: born of the sky.   5 *phantasy*:
imagination.   6 *concent*: harmony.   7 *Aye sung*: forever sung.
9 *jubilee*: rejoicing.   17 *undiscording*: not discordant, i.e. harmonizing.
18 *noise*: music; see Nativity Ode, l. 97.   19 *disproportion'd*: ugly
because misshapen. It is also implied that the introduction of sin distorted
God's plan.   20 *chime*: concord. Cf. Nativity Ode, l. 128.
22 *sway'd*: ruled.

B

In perfect diapason, whilst they stood
In first obedience, and their state of good.
O may we soon again renew that song
And keep in tune with Heaven, till God ere long
To his celestial consort us unite,
To live with him and sing in endless morn of light.

23 *diapason*: the concord of the octave (and also of the eight notes of the spheres. see Appendix 1).   27 *consort*: harmony. Cf. Nativity Ode, l. 132.

L'Allegro

HENCE, loathèd Melancholy,
  Of Cerberus and blackest Midnight born
In Stygian cave forlorn
  'Mongst horrid shapes and shrieks and sights unholy!
Find out some uncouth cell
  Where brooding Darkness spreads his jealous wings
And the night-raven sings;
  There under ebon shades and low-brow'd rocks,
As ragged as thy locks,
  In dark Cimmerian desert ever dwell.   10
But come thou Goddess fair and free,
In Heaven y-cleped Euphrosyne
And by men, heart-easing Mirth,
Whom lovely Venus at a birth
With two sister Graces more
To ivy-crownèd Bacchus bore;
Or whether (as some sager sing)
The frolic wind that breathes the spring,
Zephyr, with Aurora playing
As he met her once a-maying,   20
There on beds of violets blue
And fresh-blown roses wash'd in dew,

L'Allegro: the cheerful man.   5 *uncouth*: unknown, out-of-the-way.
shades: trees. Cf. *Comus*, ll. 62, 335.   8 *low-brow'd*: frowning.
10 *desert*: wilderness.   11 *free*: friendly. 'Fair and free' was an
ancient complimentary phrase applied to women, where 'free' carries the
sense of 'well-bred'.   12 *y-cleped*: named (an archaism in Spenser's
manner).   18 *frolic*: playful. *breathes*: inspires, fosters with its breath.
20 *a-maying*: celebrating the coming of May.

Fill'd her with thee, a daughter fair,
So buxom, blithe and debonair:
Haste thee, Nymph, and bring with thee
Jest and youthful Jollity,
Quips and Cranks and wanton Wiles,
Nods and Becks and wreathèd Smiles
Such as hang on Hebe's cheek
And love to live in dimple sleek;   30
Sport that wrinkled Care derides,
And Laughter holding both his sides.
Come, and trip it as you go
On the light fantastic toe,
And in thy right hand lead with thee
The mountain nymph, sweet Liberty;
And if I give thee honour due,
Mirth, admit me of thy crew,
To live with her and live with thee
In unreprovèd pleasures free;   40
To hear the lark begin his flight
And singing startle the dull night
From his watch-tower in the skies,
Till the dappled dawn doth rise;
Then to come in spite of sorrow
And at my window bid good-morrow
Through the sweet-briar or the vine
Or the twisted eglantine.

24 *buxom*: gracious, jolly; the original meaning was 'pliant, obedient'.
debonair: courteous (from Old French *de bon aire*, 'well-born').
27 *Quips*: witty sayings.   *Cranks*: humorous turns of phrase; the
literal meaning of *crank* is 'turn' or 'twist'.   28 *Becks*: bows, curtseys.
30 *sleek*: smooth.   31 *derides*: laughs at.   33 *trip it*: dance.
35 *in thy right hand*: held by your right hand (in the place of honour).
38 *crew*: company. See *Comus*, l. 653.   39 *her*: i.e. Liberty.   45 *in
spite of sorrow*: in defiance of.   46 *bid good-morrow*: greet the
morning.

While the cock with lively din
Scatters the rear of darkness thin,   50
And to the stack or the barn door
Stoutly struts his dames before,
Oft listening how the hounds and horn
Cheerly rouse the slumbering morn,
From the side of some hoar hill
Through the high wood echoing shrill.
Sometime walking not unseen
By hedgerow elms, on hillocks green,
Right against the eastern gate
Where the great sun begins his state   60
Robed in flames and amber light,
The clouds in thousand liveries dight;
While the ploughman near at hand
Whistles o'er the furrow'd land,
And the milkmaid singeth blithe,
And the mower whets his scythe,
And every shepherd tells his tale
Under the hawthorn in the dale.
Straight mine eye hath caught new pleasures
Whilst the lantskip round it measures: 70
Russet lawns and fallows gray
Where the nibbling flocks do stray,
Mountains on whose barren breast
The labouring clouds do often rest;

50 *Scatters the rear of darkness thin*: chases away the last shadows of the
retreating night.   52 *his dames before*: in front of his hens.   54 *Cheerly*:
cheerfully.   55 *hoar*: grey. Cf. *Arcades*, l. 98.   59 *Right against*:
directly facing.   60 *state*: triumphal progress.   62 *liveries*:
coloured costumes of servants or retainers.   *dight*: decked, arrayed.
67 *tells his tale*: numbers his flock.   69 *Straight*: at once.   70 *lantskip*:
landscape. Milton always spells the word so.   71 *Russet*: grey-brown.
lawns: grasslands. See *Lycidas*, l. 25 and Nativity Ode, l. 85.   *fallows*:
fields lying fallow, i.e. uncropped.   *gray*: light-brown.

Meadows trim with daisies pied,
Shallow brooks and rivers wide.
Towers and battlements it sees
Bosom'd high in tufted trees,
Where perhaps some beauty lies,
The Cynosure of neighbouring eyes.   80
Hard by, a cottage chimney smokes
From betwixt two agèd oaks,
Where Corydon and Thyrsis met
Are at their savoury dinner set
Of herbs and other country messes
Which the neat-handed Phillis dresses;
And then in haste her bower she leaves
With Thestylis to bind the sheaves,
Or if the earlier season lead
To the tann'd haycock in the mead.   90
Sometimes with secure delight
The upland hamlets will invite,
When the merry bells ring round
And the jocund rebecks sound
To many a youth and many a maid
Dancing in the chequer'd shade;
And young and old come forth to play
On a sunshine holiday,
Till the livelong daylight fail.
Then to the spicy nut-brown ale,   100

75 *pied*: parti-coloured, streaked.   78 *Bosom'd*: enclosed.
79 *lies*: lodges.   80 *Cynosure*: guiding star. See *Comus*, ll. 341–342 n.
83 *met*: having met.   85 *messes*: dishes.   87 *bower*: cottage
dwelling. Cf. *Comus*, l. 45; Sonnet III, l. 9.   89 *earlier season*: midsummer (before harvest). *lead*: decide.   90 *tann'd haycock*: sun-dried
heap of hay.   91 *secure*: carefree.   94 *rebecks*: fiddles of four
strings.   98 *sunshine holiday*: holiday at a sunny time of year. Cf.
Comus, l. 959.

With stories told of many a feat:
How fairy Mab the junkets eat;
She was pinch'd and pull'd, she said,
And he by Friar's Lantern led,
Tells how the drudging goblin sweat
To earn his cream-bowl duly set,
When in one night, ere glimpse of morn,
His shadowy flail hath thresh'd the corn
That ten day-labourers could not end;
Then lies him down the lubber fiend,   110
And stretch'd out all the chimney's length,
Basks at the fire his hairy strength,
And crop-full out of doors he flings
Ere the first cock his matin rings.
Thus done the tales, to bed they creep,
By whispering winds soon lull'd asleep.
Tower'd cities please us then,
And the busy hum of men,
Where throngs of knights and barons bold
In weeds of peace high triumphs hold,   120
With store of ladies whose bright eyes
Rain influence, and judge the prize
Of wit or arms, while both contend
To win her grace whom all commend.
There let Hymen oft appear
In saffron robe, with taper clear,

102 *junkets*: food made from milk.   103 *She*: i.e. the girl telling
the story to the company.   104 *he*: another speaker who tells his
adventure.   105 *drudging*: hard-working.   108 *shadowy*:
ghostly.   109 *end*: come to the end of.   110 *lubber*: big, ungainly.
fiend: spirit.   111 *chimney's*: hearth's.   113 *crop-full*: full-fed.
114 *matin*: morning prayer or hymn.   120 *weeds*: garments.   *triumphs*:
processions, pageants.   121 *store*: plenty.   122 *influence*: starry
radiance. See Nativity Ode, l. 71 n.

And pomp and feast and revelry,
With masque and antique pageantry:
Such sights as youthful poets dream
On summer eves by haunted stream.   130
Then to the well-trod stage anon,
If Jonson's learnèd sock be on,
Or sweetest Shakespeare, Fancy's child,
Warble his native wood-notes wild.
And ever against eating cares
Lap me in soft Lydian airs
Married to immortal verse,
Such as the meeting soul may pierce
In notes with many a winding bout
Of linkèd sweetness long drawn out,   140
With wanton heed and giddy cunning
The melting voice through mazes running,
Untwisting all the chains that tie
The hidden soul of harmony:
That Orpheus' self may heave his head
From golden slumber on a bed
Of heap'd Elysian flowers, and hear
Such strains as would have won the ear
Of Pluto, to have quite set free
His half-regain'd Eurydice.   150
These delights if thou canst give,
Mirth, with thee I mean to live.

127 *pomp*: procession or pageant.   *revelry*: theatrical or musical
entertainments.   128 *antique*: grotesque.   131 *well-trod*: 'implies the
skill of the actor' (Wright).   *anon*: swiftly.   135 *eating*: gnawing.
136 *Lap me*: wrap me.   138 *the meeting soul*: i.e. the soul responding
eagerly to the music.   *pierce*: penetrate.   139 *bout*: bend, round
(here a stretch or movement of music).   141 *heed*: attention.   *cun-*
ning: skill. Attention and skill which are 'wanton' and 'giddy' describe
the paradox of artistic inspiration.

Il Penseroso

HENCE, vain deluding joys,
  The brood of folly without father bred,
How little you bestead
  Or fill the fixèd mind with all your toys!
Dwell in some idle brain,
  And fancies fond with gaudy shapes possess,
As thick and numberless
  As the gay motes that people the sunbeams,
Or likest hovering dreams,
  The fickle pensioners of Morpheus' train.   10
But hail thou Goddess sage and holy,
Hail, divinest Melancholy,
Whose saintly visage is too bright
To hit the sense of human sight,
And therefore to our weaker view
O'erlaid with black, staid Wisdom's hue:
Black, but such as in esteem
Prince Memnon's sister might beseem,
Or that starr'd Ethiop queen that strove
To set her beauty's praise above   20
The sea-nymphs, and their powers offended.
Yet thou art higher far descended:
Thee bright-hair'd Vesta long of yore
To solitary Saturn bore,

Il Penseroso: the thoughtful man.   3 *bestead*: help. Cf. *Comus*, l. 611.
4 *fixèd*: firmly settled. *toys*: trifles.   6 *fond*: foolish. *gaudy*: festive.
Cf. Nativity Ode, l. 33. *possess*: occupy.   10 *pensioners*: retainers.
train: suite.   14 *hit*: meet or agree with.   16 *staid*: sober.
18 *beseem*: become, suit.   22 *higher far*: much more highly.

His daughter she (in Saturn's reign
Such mixture was not held a stain);
Oft in glimmering bowers and glades
He met her, and in secret shades
Of woody Ida's inmost grove,
While yet there was no fear of Jove.   30
Come, pensive nun, devout and pure,
Sober, steadfast and demure,
All in a robe of darkest grain
Flowing with majestic train,
And sable stole of cypress lawn
Over thy decent shoulders drawn.
Come, but keep thy wonted state,
With even step and musing gait
And looks commercing with the skies,
Thy rapt soul sitting in thine eyes: 40
There held in holy passion still,
Forget thyself to marble, till
With a sad leaden downward cast
Thou fix them on the earth as fast.
And join with thee calm Peace and Quiet,
Spare Fast, that oft with gods doth diet
And hears the Muses in a ring

26 *mixture*: incestuous love.   *held a stain*: considered a sin.   33 *grain*:
colour (from the seeds used to make certain dyes). See *Comus*, l. 750.
35 *sable stole*: black veil or scarf.   *cypress lawn*: black thin transparent
material.   36 *decent*: well dressed.   37 *wonted state*: customary
solemnity.   38 *musing gait*: slow walk of one who is thinking.
39 *commercing with the skies*: looking to Heaven for inspiration (i.e. the
eyes look up and the sky looks down).   41 *holy passion*: devoted love
of God.   *still*: unmoving.   42 *Forget thyself to marble*: 'be so lost in
thought that you are still as a statue'.   43 *cast*: dropping of the eyes.
44 'You fix your eyes as firmly on the earth as before on Heaven.'
45 *join*: unite.   46 *Spare*: frugal. See *Comus*, l. 767.   *diet*: eat, i.e.
board.

Aye round about Jove's altar sing;
And add to these retirèd Leisure
That in trim gardens takes his pleasure.   50
But first and chiefest, with thee bring
Him that yon soars on golden wing,
Guiding the fiery-wheelèd throne,
The Cherub Contemplation;
And the mute Silence hist along,
'Less Philomel will deign a song,
In her sweetest, saddest plight
Smoothing the rugged brow of Night,
While Cynthia checks her dragon yoke
Gently o'er the accustom'd oak.   60
Sweet bird that shunn'st the noise of folly,
Most musical, most melancholy!
Thee, chauntress, oft the woods among,
I woo to hear thy even-song;
And missing thee, I walk unseen
On the dry smooth-shaven green,
To behold the wandering moon
Riding near her highest noon,
Like one that had been led astray
Through the Heaven's wide pathless way,   70
And oft, as if her head she bow'd,
Stooping through a fleecy cloud.
Oft on a plat of rising ground
I hear the far-off curfew sound
Over some wide-water'd shore,

48 *Aye*: forever.   49 *retirèd*: secluded.   54 *Contemplation*: accent
'Contemplati–on'.   55 *hist along*: whisper to come along.   56 *'Less*:
unless.   57 *plight*: mood.   59 *checks*: reins in.   *yoke*: pair of yoked
animals.   63 *chauntress*: songstress.   64 *woo*: seek out.   68 *highest noon*:
the meridian of the moon's course.   73 *plat*: open space.   75 *shore*:
land bordering on water, or the shallow waters near it. Cf. *Lycidas*, l. 154.

Swinging slow with sullen roar;
Or if the air will not permit,
Some still removèd place will fit,
Where glowing embers through the room
Teach light to counterfeit a gloom,   80
Far from all resort of mirth
Save the cricket on the hearth,
Or the bellman's drowsy charm
To bless the doors from nightly harm.
Or let my lamp at midnight hour
Be seen in some high lonely tower,
Where I may oft outwatch the Bear
With thrice-great Hermes, or unsphere
The spirit of Plato, to unfold
What worlds or what vast regions hold   90
The immortal mind that hath forsook
Her mansion in this fleshly nook;
And of those daemons that are found
In fire, air, flood, or under ground,
Whose power hath a true consent
With planet or with element.
Sometime let gorgeous Tragedy
In sceptred pall come sweeping by,
Presenting Thebes, or Pelops' line,

77 *air*: weather.   78 *removèd*: remote.   *will fit*: will suit my purpose.   80 *counterfeit*: imitate, feign.   83 *bellman*: night-watchman.
drowsy charm: song causing sleep (called a charm because it seems to exor-
cize danger).   84 *nightly harm*: harm by night.   87 *outwatch*:
keep awake longer than.   88 *unsphere*: draw down from its sphere.
89 *unfold*: discover.   92 *mansion*: dwelling.   *fleshly nook*: bodily
abode ('nook' implies the lowliness and smallness of the body as a house
for the soul).   93 *daemons*: spirits (not necessarily evil).   95 *consent*:
harmony. Cf. *At a Solemn Music*, l. 6.   97 *Sometime*: sometimes.
gorgeous: stately in dress.   98 *sceptred*: regal.   *pall*: cloak or mantle.
99 *line*: royal family.

Or the tale of Troy divine,   100
Or what (though rare) of later age
Ennobled hath the buskin'd stage.
But O sad virgin, that thy power
Might raise Musaeus from his bower,
Or bid the soul of Orpheus sing
Such notes as, warbled to the string,
Drew iron tears down Pluto's cheek
And made Hell grant what Love did seek;
Or call up him that left half told
The story of Cambuscan bold,   110
Of Camball and of Algarsife,
And who had Canace to wife
That own'd the virtuous ring and glass,
And of the wondrous horse of brass
On which the Tartar king did ride;
And if aught else great bards beside
In sage and solemn tunes have sung,
Of tourneys and of trophies hung,
Of forests and enchantments drear,
Where more is meant than meets the ear.   120
Thus, Night, oft see me in thy pale career
Till civil-suited Morn appear,
Not trick'd and frounced as she was wont
With the Attic boy to hunt,
But kerchief'd in a comely cloud,

102 *buskin'd stage*: i.e. tragic theatre.   104 *bower*: secret dwelling-
place. Cf. *Comus*, l. 45, *L'Allegro*, l. 87.   106 *warbled*: sung. Cf.
Nativity Ode, l. 96, *Arcades* l. 87.   113 *virtuous*: possessing magic
powers. See *Comus*, l. 621.   116 *beside*: in addition.   119 *drear*:
sinister. See *Comus*, l. 37.   121 *career*: course. See Sonnet II, l. 3.
122 *civil-suited*: soberly dressed.   123 *trick'd*: adorned. Cf. *Lycidas*,
l. 170.   *frounced*: with curled hair.   125 *kerchief'd*: with hair tied
up in a kerchief.

While rocking winds are piping loud,
Or usher'd with a shower still
When the gust hath blown his fill,
Ending on the rustling leaves
With minute-drops from off the eaves.   130
And when the sun begins to fling
His flaring beams, me, Goddess, bring
To archèd walks of twilight groves
And shadows brown that Sylvan loves,
Of pine or monumental oak,
Where the rude axe with heavèd stroke
Was never heard the nymphs to daunt
Or fright them from their hallow'd haunt.
There is close covert by some brook
Where no profaner eye may look,   140
Hide me from Day's garish eye
While the bee with honey'd thigh,
That at her flowery work doth sing,
And the waters murmuring
With such consort as they keep,
Entice the dewy-feather'd sleep;
And let some strange mysterious dream
Wave at his wings, in airy stream
Of lively portraiture display'd,
Softly on my eyelids laid.   150
And as I wake, sweet music breathe

126 *rocking*: causing the trees or waves to rock.   *piping*: whistling.
127 *usher'd*: announced. *still*: quiet.   130 *minute-drops*: drops falling at
intervals of a minute.   134 *brown*: dark. Cf. *Lycidas*, l. 2.   135 *monumental*: massive and lasting.   136 *rude*: rough.   *heavèd*: lifted.
140 *profaner*: more familiar, less respectful.   141 *garish*: staring.
145 *consort*: harmony. Cf. Nativity Ode, l. 132.   148 *Wave at his
wings*: come fluttering on the wings of sleep.   148–9 'displaying
itself in a stream of lively images'.   151 *sweet music breathe*: 'let sweet
music breathe'.

Above, about or underneath,
Sent by some spirit to mortals good,
Or the unseen Genius of the wood.
But let my due feet never fail
To walk the studious cloister's pale,
And love the high embowèd roof
With antic pillars massy proof,
And storied windows richly dight
Casting a dim religious light.   160
There let the pealing organ blow
To the full-voiced quire below,
In service high and anthems clear
As may with sweetness, through mine ear,
Dissolve me into ecstasies
And bring all Heaven before mine eyes.
And may at last my weary age
Find out the peaceful hermitage,
The hairy gown and mossy cell,
Where I may sit and rightly spell   170
Of every star that Heaven doth shew,
And every herb that sips the dew;
Till old experience do attain
To something like prophetic strain.
These pleasures, Melancholy, give,
And I with thee will choose to live.

153 *to mortals good*: well disposed to men.   154 *Genius*: divinity.
Cf. *Arcades*, ll. 43–80; Nativity Ode, l. 186 and *Lycidas*, l. 183.   155 *due
feet*: feet doing what they should, i.e. obedient.   156 *pale*: enclosure.
studious: favourable to study.   157 *embowèd*: vaulted.   158 *antic*:
grotesquely carved. Cf. *L'Allegro*, l. 128. *massy proof*: unshakably massive.
159 *storied*: ornamented with histories or legends. *dight*: adorned. Cf.
L'Allegro, l. 62.   163 *high*: stately.   170 *spell*: interpret. Cf.
Sonnet VI, l. 7.   175 *prophetic strain*: the poem of a prophet.

Arcades

Part of an Entertainment presented to the Countess Dowager of Derby at Harefield by some noble persons of her family, who appear on the Scene in pastoral habit, moving toward the seat of state, with this Song:

I. SONG

LOOK Nymphs, and Shepherds look,
What sudden blaze of majesty
Is that which we from hence descry,
Too divine to be mistook:
  This, this is she
To whom our vows and wishes bend,
Here our solemn search hath end.

Fame that her high worth to raise
Seem'd erst so lavish and profuse,
We may justly now accuse   10
Of detraction from her praise;
  Less than half we find express'd,
  Envy bid conceal the rest.

Mark what radiant state she spreads
In circle round her shining throne,
Shooting her beams like silver threads:
This, this is she alone,

admiratio

Arcades: Arcadians. Pronounce 'Arcad-es'.   *seat of state*: a raised chair or throne, to be occupied by the person of highest rank in an assembly. Cf. *Comus*, l. 35 n.   6 *To whom our vows and wishes bend*: 'Whom we have desired and prayed to find'.   *vows*: prayers. Cf. *Lycidas*, l. 159. 9 *erst*: at one time.   14 *state*: pomp. Cf. *L'Allegro*, l. 60.

Sitting like a goddess bright
In the centre of her light.

Might she the wise Latona be,   20
Or the tow'rèd Cybele,
Mother of a hundred gods?
Juno dares not give her odds;
  Who had thought this clime had held
  A deity so unparallel'd?

As they come forward, the Genius of the Wood *appears, and
turning toward them, speaks.*

Gen. Stay, gentle swains, for though in this disguise,
I see bright honour sparkle through your eyes;
Of famous Arcady ye are, and sprung
Of that renownèd flood, so often sung,
Divine Alpheus, who by secret sluice   30
Stole under seas to meet his Arethuse;
And ye, the breathing roses of the wood,
Fair silver-buskin'd Nymphs as great and good,
I know this quest of yours and free intent
Was all in honour and devotion meant
To the great mistress of yon princely shrine,
Whom with low reverence I adore as mine,
And with all helpful service will comply
To further this night's glad solemnity,

21 *tow'rèd*: crowned with towers.   23 *give her odds*: make allowance to her as an inferior.   24 *this clime*: this region of the earth. Cf.
Comus, l. 977 and Sonnet III, l. 8.   26 *gentle*: well-born.   *swains*:
country labourers.   27 *honour*: nobility.   30 *sluice*: channel.
33 *as great and good*: i.e. as the 'swains'.   34 *quest*: hunt (i.e. the search
for the Countess). *free intent*: gracious purpose.   37 *as mine*: i.e. as
my mistress.   39 *solemnity*: celebration. See *Comus*, ll. 142, 746.

And lead ye where ye may more near behold   40
What shallow-searching Fame hath left untold;
Which I full oft amidst these shades alone
Have sat to wonder at, and gaze upon.
For know, by lot from Jove I am the Power
Of this fair wood, and live in oaken bower,
To nurse the saplings tall, and curl the grove
With ringlets quaint, and wanton windings wove.
And all my plants I save from nightly ill
Of noisome winds and blasting vapours chill,
And from the boughs brush off the evil dew,   50
And heal the harms of thwarting thunder blue,
Or what the cross dire-looking planet smites,
Or hurtful worm with canker'd venom bites.
When evening gray doth rise, I fetch my round
Over the mount and all this hallow'd ground,
And early, ere the odorous breath of morn
Awakes the slumbering leaves, or tassell'd horn
Shakes the high thicket, haste I all about,
Number my ranks, and visit every sprout
With puissant words and murmurs made to bless.   60
But else in deep of night, when drowsiness
Hath lock'd up mortal sense, then listen I
To the celestial Sirens' harmony,

41 *shallow-searching*: looking superficially. *Fame*: rumour.   44 *by
lot*: as my assignment. Cf. *Comus*, l. 20.   *Power*: local divinity.
45 *bower*: see *Comus*, l. 46.   47 *quaint*: intricate. Cf. Nativity Ode,
l. 194. *wanton*: luxuriant. *wove*: woven.   48 *nightly ill*: harm by
night. Cf. *Il Penseroso*, l. 84.   49 *noisome*: troublesome. *blasting*:
blighting.   51 *thwarting*: striking athwart, or criss-cross. *thunder
blue*: blue lightning.   52 *cross dire-looking*: looking askance and sinister.
53 *canker'd*: infected with blight.   54 *fetch my round*: make my round.
55 *hallow'd ground*: cf. *Il Penseroso*, l. 138.   57 *tassell'd horn*: hunting horn.   58 *all about*: all round (my domain).   60 *puissant*:
potent (i.e. of magic power). *murmurs*: spells. Cf. *Comus*, l. 526.

That sit upon the nine infolded spheres
And sing to those that hold the vital shears
And turn the adamantine spindle round,
On which the fate of gods and men is wound:
Such sweet compulsion doth in music lie,
To lull the daughters of Necessity,
And keep unsteady Nature to her law,   70
And the low world in measured motion draw
After the heavenly tune, which none can hear
Of human mould, with gross unpurgèd ear.
And yet such music worthiest were to blaze
The peerless height of her immortal praise
Whose lustre leads us, and for her most fit,
If my inferior hand or voice could hit
Inimitable sounds. Yet as we go,
Whate'er the skill of lesser gods can show
I will assay, her worth to celebrate,   80
And so attend ye toward her glittering state;
Where ye may all that are of noble stem
Approach, and kiss her sacred vesture's hem.

64 *infolded*: i.e. concentric, each enfolding one smaller than itself, and
enfolded by one larger.   65 *the vital shears*: the shears of life.
70 *unsteady*: changeable.   71 *measured*: rhythmical.   73 *mould*:
both shape and substance. Cf. *Comus*, l. 17.   *unpurgèd*: unpurified.
74 *were*: would be.   *blaze*: proclaim. Cf. *Lycidas*, l. 74.   76 *lustre*:
glory   *leads us*: attracts us.   77 *hit*: reach. Cf. *Il Penseroso*, l. 14,
and *Comus*, l. 286.   78 *go*: move (towards her).   80 *assay*: attempt.
81 *attend ye*: accompany you.   *state*: throne. See *Comus*, l. 35.   82 *stem*:
stock.

II. SONG

O'er the smooth enamell'd green
Where no print of step hath been,
    Follow me as I sing
    And touch the warbled string.
Under the shady roof
Of branching elm star-proof,
    Follow me: 90
I will bring you where she sits
Clad in splendour as befits
    Her deity.
Such a rural Queen
All Arcadia hath not seen.

III. SONG

Nymphs and Shepherds, dance no more
    By sandy Ladon's lilied banks;
On old Lycaeus or Cyllene hoar
    Trip no more in twilight ranks;
Though Erymanth your loss deplore,   100
    A better soil shall give ye thanks.
From the stony Maenalus
Bring your flocks, and live with us;
Here ye shall have greater grace,
To serve the Lady of this place.
Though Syrinx your Pan's mistress were,
Yet Syrinx well might wait on her;
    Such a rural Queen
    All Arcadia hath not seen.

84 *enamell'd*: bright in colour as enamel.   87 *warbled string*: cf·
Nativity Ode, ll. 96–7, and *Il Penseroso*, l. 106.   89 *star-proof*: too thick to
be pierced by the light of the stars.   93 *deity*: godlikeness (i.e. a title, as
in 'her Majesty').   98 *Cyllene*: Pronounce as two syllables *hoar*:
grey or white headed (with snow).   104 *grace*: reward.

Comus

A MASQUE PRESENTED AT LUDLOW CASTLE, 1634

To the Right Honourable John, Lord Viscount Brackley, son and heir-apparent to the Earl of Bridgewater, etc.

MY LORD,

This poem, which received its first occasion of birth from yourself and others of your noble family, and much honour from your own person in the performance, now returns again to make a final dedication of itself to you. Although not openly acknowledged by the Author, yet it is a legitimate offspring, so lovely and so much desired, that the often copying of it hath tired my pen to give my several friends satisfaction, and brought me to a necessity 10 of producing it to the public view; and now to offer it up, in all rightful devotion, to those fair hopes and rare endowments of your much-promising youth, which give a full assurance to all that know you of a future excellence. Live, sweet Lord, to be the honour of your name; and receive this as your own from the hands of him who hath by many favours been long obliged to your most honoured Parents, and, as in this representation your attendant Thyrsis, so now in all real expression 20

Your faithful and most humble Servant,
H. LAWES[1]

[1] From the edition of 1637; it was reprinted by Milton in the edition of 1645.

The Copy of a Letter written by Sir Henry Wotton to the Author, upon the following Poem

From the College, this 13 of April, 1638

SIR,

It was a special favour when you lately bestowed upon me here the first taste of your acquaintance, though no longer than to make me know that I wanted more time to value it and to enjoy it rightly; and, in truth, if I could then have imagined your farther stay in these parts, which I understood afterwards by Mr H., I would have been so bold, in our vulgar phrase, to mend my draught (for you left me with an extreme thirst), and to have begged your conversation again, jointly with your said learned friend, at a poor meal or two, that we might have banded together some good Authors of the ancient time; among which I observed you to have been familiar.

Since your going, you have charged me with new obligations, both for a very kind letter from you dated the 6th of this month, and for a dainty piece of entertainment which came therewith. Wherein I should much commend the tragical part, if the lyrical did not ravish me with a certain Doric delicacy in your Songs and Odes, whereunto I must plainly confess to have seen yet nothing parallel in our language: *Ipsa mollities*. But I must not omit to tell you that I now only owe you thanks for intimating unto me (how modestly soever) the true artificer. For the work itself I had viewed some good while before with singular delight; having received it from our common friend Mr R., in the very close of the late R.'s Poems, printed at Oxford: whereunto it was added (as I now suppose) that

33 *mend my draught*: drink again, i.e. completely quench my thirst. 36 *banded*: bandied, discussed. 43 *tragical*: dramatic. 44 *Doric*: pastoral. See *Lycidas*, l. 189 n. 46 *Ipsa mollities*: i.e. smoothness itself.

the accessory might help out the principal, according to the art of Stationers, and to leave the reader *con la bocca dolce*.

Now, Sir, concerning your travels; wherein I may challenge a little more privilege of discourse with you. I suppose you will not blanch Paris in your way: therefore I have been bold to trouble you with a few lines to Mr M. B., whom you shall easily find attending the young Lord S. as his governor; and you may surely receive from 60 him good directions for the shaping of your farther journey into Italy, where he did reside, by my choice, some time for the King, after mine own recess from Venice.

I should think that your best line will be through the whole length of France to Marseilles, and thence by sea to Genoa; whence the passage into Tuscany is as diurnal as a Gravesend barge. I hasten, as you do, to Florence or Siena, the rather to tell you a short story, from the interest you have given me in your safety.

At Siena I was tabled in the house of one Alberto Scipioni, 70 an old Roman courtier in dangerous times; having been steward to the Duca di Pagliano, who with all his family were strangled, save this only man that escaped by fore-sight of the tempest. With him I had often much chat of those affairs, into which he took pleasure to look back from his native harbour; and at my departure toward Rome (which had been the centre of his experience), I had won confidence enough to beg his advice how I might carry myself securely there without offence of others or of mine own conscience. '*Signor Arrigo mio*,' says he, '*i pensieri* 80 *stretti ed il viso sciolto* will go safely over the whole world.'

---

54 *con la bocca dolce*: with a sweet taste in the mouth.   57 *blanch*: omit.   63 *recess*: retirement.   80 *Signor Arrigo mio*: 'Master Harry, my friend'   80-1 *i pensieri … sciolto*: 'your thoughts kept to yourself and your countenance open to all.'

Of which Delphian oracle (for so I have found it) your judgment doth need no commentary; and therefore, Sir, I will commit you with it to the best of all securities, God's dear love, remaining

Your friend, as much at command as any of longer date,

HENRY WOTTON

Postscript

Sir: I have expressly sent this my footboy to prevent 90 your departure without some acknowledgement from me of the receipt of your obliging letter; having myself through some business, I know not how, neglected the ordinary conveyance. In any part where I shall understand you fixed, I shall be glad and diligent to entertain you with home-novelties, even for some fomentation of our friendship, too soon interrupted in the cradle.

THE PERSONS

The Attendant Spirit, afterwards in the habit of *Thyrsis*.
Comus, with his Crew.
The Lady.
First Brother.
Second Brother.
Sabrina, the Nymph.

The Chief Persons which presented were:

The Lord Brackley;
Mr Thomas Egerton, his Brother;
The Lady Alice Egerton.

96 *fomentation*: fostering.

COMUS

The first Scene discovers a wild wood.
The Attendant Spirit *descends or enters.*

BEFORE the starry threshold of Jove's court
My mansion is, where those immortal shapes
Of bright aereal spirits live insphered
In regions mild of calm and serene air,
Above the smoke and stir of this dim spot
Which men call Earth, and with low-thoughted care
Confined and pester'd in this pinfold here,
Strive to keep up a frail and feverish being
Unmindful of the crown that Virtue gives
After this mortal change, to her true servants   10
Amongst the enthroned gods on sainted seats.
Yet some there be that by due steps aspire
To lay their just hands on that golden key
That opes the palace of Eternity:
To such my errand is, and but for such
I would not soil these pure ambrosial weeds

(Stage Direction) *discovers*: reveals.   2 *mansion*: dwelling-place.
4 *serene*: clear. Accent 'sèrene'.   6 *low-thoughted care*: preoccupation
with inferior objects or ambitions. 'Men', having been introduced as the
subject of a relative clause, becomes the subject of a main clause that follows.
7 *pester'd*: hampered. To 'pester' originally meant to hobble with a foot-
shackle a horse put out to graze. Here the sense of 'tethered or hindered' is
combined with the idea of being crowded together.   *pinfold*: a pound or
pen for cattle.   8 *being*: existence.   9 *unmindful of*: not caring for.
10 *this mortal change*: i.e. life. See also l. 841.   11 *enthroned*: Accent
'ènthroned'.   *gods*: spirits.   12 *due*: appropriate.   16 *ambrosial weeds*: heavenly garments. 'Ambrosial' in Greek meant immortal
or fresh; hence it was applied to the food or clothes of the Gods
and acquired the meaning of sweet or fragrant. See l. 840. For 'weeds' see
also ll. 84, 189.

With the rank vapours of this sin-worn mould.
But to my task. Neptune, besides the sway
Of every salt flood and each ebbing stream,
Took in by lot 'twixt high and nether Jove   20
Imperial rule of all the sea-girt isles
That like to rich and various gems inlay
The unadornèd bosom of the deep;
Which he to grace his tributary gods
By course commits to several government,
And gives them leave to wear their sapphire crowns
And wield their little tridents. But this isle,
The greatest and the best of all the main,
He quarters to his blue-hair'd deities;
And all this tract that fronts the falling sun   30
A noble Peer of mickle trust and power
Has in his charge, with temper'd awe to guide
An old and haughty nation, proud in arms:
Where his fair offspring, nursed in princely lore,
Are coming to attend their father's state
And new-entrusted sceptre. But their way

17 *rank*: evil-smelling. Cf. *Lycidas*, l. 126.   *mould*: clay or earth of
which man is made. Cf. l. 244 and Nativity Ode, l. 138. 'Mould'
can be used to mean either the substance or the shape it takes.
18 *sway*: control, government.   20 *Took in*: included.   *by lot*:
as his allotment.   22 *various*: contrasting.   24 *Which*: i.e. the
isles.   *grace*: give honours to.   *tributary*: subordinate.   25 *By
course*: 'in turn' or 'as time goes on'.   *several government*: separate
government, i.e. one to each minor deity.   26 *them*: the lesser
gods.   29 *quarters*: allots as a portion (from dividing into four parts).
30 *fronts*: faces.   *falling*: sinking.   31 *mickle*: great.   *trust*: delegated authority.   32 *temper'd awe*: dignity moderated by kindness.
guide: govern.   33 *proud in arms*: famous for their success in war.
34 *nursed in princely lore*: educated as rulers should be.   35 *attend*:
be present at.   *state*: throne. Here it indicates the ceremony of installation as Lord President. Cf. *Arcades*, 'seat of state'.   36 *new-entrusted
sceptre*: power newly delegated (by the king).

Lies through the perplex'd paths of this drear wood, *maze*
The nodding horror of whose shady brows
Threats the forlorn and wandering passenger.
And here their tender age might suffer peril,   40
But that by quick command from sovran Jove
I was despatch'd for their defence and guard; *MASTER OF MAZE*
And listen why, for I will tell ye now
What never yet was heard in tale or song   *original*
From old or modern bard, in hall or bower.
  Bacchus, that first from out the purple grape
Crush'd the sweet poison of misusèd wine,   *wine*
After the Tuscan mariners transform'd
Coasting the Tyrrhene shore, as the winds listed,   *drunkenness*
On Circe's island fell (who knows not Circe   50
The daughter of the sun, whose charmèd cup   *Comus*
Whoever tasted lost his upright shape,   *Orpheus*
And downward fell into a grovelling swine?).   *like*
This Nymph, that gazed upon his clustering locks   *Caliban*
With ivy berries wreath'd, and his blithe youth,
Had by him, ere he parted thence, a son
Much like his father, but his mother more,
Whom therefore she brought up, and Comus named:
Who ripe, and frolic of his full-grown age,

---

37 *perplex'd*: tangled. Accent 'pèrplex'd'.   38 *horror*: roughness (Lat. *horror*). Cf. *horrid*, l. 429. The ragged waving branches are compared to dark locks of hair nodding on a scowling forehead.   39 *forlorn*: lost. *passenger*: traveller.   41 *sovran*: sovereign.   45 *hall or bower*: In a medieval castle, the hall was the large room for public entertainment, the bower a more private apartment associated with the ladies of the house. The minstrel might sing in either.   48 'After the transformation of the Tuscan mariners.' The construction is Latin, but was echoed in the titles of Renaissance epics: *Gerusalemme Liberata, Paradise Lost*.   *Tuscan*: Italian. See Sonnet XVI, l. 12.   49 *listed*: willed.   50 *On . . . fell*: chanced on.   51 *charmèd*: enchanted.   59 *Who ripe*: who having grown up.   *frolic*: pleasure-seeking.   *of*: because of.

Roving the Celtic and Iberian fields,   60
At last betakes him to this ominous wood,
And in thick shelter of black shades imbower'd
Excels his mother at her mighty art,
Offering to every weary traveller
His orient liquor in a crystal glass
To quench the drouth of Phoebus; which as they taste
(For most do taste through fond intemperate thirst)
Soon as the potion works, their human count'nance,
Th'express resemblance of the gods, is changed
Into some brutish form of wolf or bear   70
Or ounce or tiger, hog or bearded goat,
All other parts remaining as they were;
And they, so perfect is their misery,
Not once perceive their foul disfigurement,
But boast themselves more comely than before,
And all their friends and native home forget,
To roll with pleasure in a sensual sty.
Therefore when any favour'd of high Jove
Chances to pass through this advent'rous glade,
Swift as the sparkle of a glancing star   80
I shoot from Heav'n to give him safe convoy,
As now I do. But first I must put off
These my sky-robes spun out of Iris' woof,

---

60 *fields*: plains.   61 *ominous*: dangerous.   62 *imbower'd*:
enclosed.   63 *mighty art*: powerful magic.   65 *orient*: bright;
literally, 'eastern'. Gems came from the East, the sun rises there;
hence the meaning 'bright or brilliant'.   66 *drouth of Phoebus*: thirst
caused by the sun.   67 *fond*: foolish.   69 *express*: clearly stamped.
71 *ounce*: a kind of lynx.   73 *perfect*: complete. *misery*: abasement.
75 *boast themselves more comely*: 'are proud because they think themselves
more handsome'.   78 *favour'd of*: loved by.   79 *advent'rous*: full of
adventures, i.e. hazards.   81 *safe convoy*: safe conduct. Accent 'convòy'.
83 *These my sky-robes*: these garments I wear in Heaven.   *spun out of Iris'*
woof: 'woven from threads provided by the goddess Iris (i.e. the rainbow)'

And take the weeds and likeness of a swain
That to the service of this house belongs,
Who with his soft pipe and smooth-dittied song
Well knows to still the wild winds when they roar,
And hush the waving woods; nor of less faith,
And in this office of his mountain watch
Likeliest, and nearest to the present aid   90
Of this occasion. But I hear the tread
Of hateful steps; I must be viewless now.

*Comus enters with a charming-rod in one hand, his glass in
the other; with him a rout of monsters, headed like sundry sorts
of wild beasts, but otherwise like men and women. Their
apparel glistering, they come in making a riotous and unruly
noise, with torches in their hands.*

Comus. The star that bids the shepherd fold
Now the top of Heaven doth hold,
And the gilded car of day
His glowing axle doth allay
In the steep Atlantic stream,
And the slope sun his upward beam
Shoots against the dusky Pole,
Pacing toward the other goal   100

84 *weeds and likeness*: clothes and appearance.   *swain*: countryman.   86 *smooth-dittied song*: song with smooth words.   87 *Well
knows to*: knows well how to.   88 *nor of less faith*: 'and his
fidelity is no less than his skill'.   89 *office*: duty.   *mountain watch*:
watching on the hills, i.e. as a shepherd.   90 *Likeliest*: most skilful.
90–1 *nearest . . . occasion*: 'the nearest help in the present emergency'.
92 *viewless*: unseen.   (Stage Direction) *charming-rod*: a magician's
wand.   *rout*: rabble, pack.   93 *fold*: lead his flock to the sheepfold
(at evening).   94 i.e. has risen to the meridian.   96 *allay*: cool.
97 *steep*: deep, i.e. far off from land.   *stream*: the ocean stream.
98 *slope*: 'aslant, on an inclined course' (Wright).   100 *Pacing*:
running his course.   *other goal*: opposite goal.

Of his chamber in the East.
Meanwhile welcome joy and feast,
Midnight shout and revelry,
Tipsy dance and jollity.
Braid your locks with rosy twine
Dropping odours, dropping wine.
Rigour now is gone to bed,
And Advice with scrupulous head,
Strict Age and sour Severity,
With their grave saws in slumber lie.   110
We that are of purer fire
Imitate the starry quire,
Who in their nightly watchful spheres
Lead in swift round the months and years.
The sounds and seas with all their finny drove
Now to the moon in wavering morrice move,
And on the tawny sands and shelves
Trip the pert fairies and the dapper elves;
By dimpled brook and fountain brim
The wood-nymphs deck'd with daisies trim,   120
Their merry wakes and pastimes keep:
What hath night to do with sleep?
Night hath better sweets to prove;
Venus now wakes, and wakens Love.
Come let us our rites begin,
'Tis only daylight that makes sin,

105 *rosy twine*: wreathed roses.   106 *Dropping*: shedding, dripping
with.   *odours*: perfume.   107 *Rigour*: strictness.   108 *scrupulous head*:
prudent thoughts. The phrase suggests wise wagging of the head.
110 *saws*: sayings, maxims.   113 *nightly watchful*: keeping watch by
night.   114 *round*: circular dance. See l. 144.   115 *sounds and seas*:
narrow and open seas.   *finny drove*: shoals of fish.   116 *morrice*:
morris-dance.   117 *shelves*: shores.   118 *pert*: brisk.   *dapper*:
neatly dressed.   121 *wakes . . . keep*: hold revels by night.   123 *sweets
to prove*: pleasures to taste.   125 *rites*: festivities.

Which these dun shades will ne'er report.
Hail goddess of nocturnal sport,
Dark-veil'd Cotytto, t'whom the secret flame
Of midnight torches burns! mysterious dame   130
That ne'er art call'd but when the dragon womb
Of Stygian darkness spets her thickest gloom
And makes one blot of all the air:
Stay thy cloudy ebon chair
Wherein thou ridest with Hecat, and befriend
Us the vow'd priests, till utmost end
Of all thy dues be done, and none left out,
Ere the blabbing eastern scout,
The nice Morn on the Indian steep
From her cabin'd loop-hole peep,   140
And to the tell-tale Sun descry
Our conceal'd solemnity.
Come, knit hands, and beat the ground
In a light fantastic round.

The Measure.

Break off, break off! I feel the different pace
Of some chaste footing near about this ground.
Run to your shrouds, within these brakes and trees;
Our number may affright. Some virgin sure

128 *sport*: gaiety.   130 *dame*: lady or queen.   131 *ne'er . . .
but when*: only when.   132 *spets*: spits out.   134 *stay*: halt. *ebon*:
ebony. *chair*: chariot.   136 *vow'd priests*: priests dedicated by vows.
utmost end: complete performance.   137 *dues*: rites due to the goddess.   138 *blabbing*: talkative, indiscreet. *scout*: spy (for the coming
sun).   139 *nice*: squeamish. *steep*: mountain range.   140 *cabin'd*
loop-hole: narrow space or slit through which to peep.   141 *descry*:
describe.   142 *solemnity*: festival. See *Arcades*, l. 39.   (Stage
Direction) *The Measure*: a stately dance (here burlesqued by the crew of
monsters).   147 *shrouds*: hiding-places. *brakes*: thickets.   148 *sure*:
for sure.

(For so I can distinguish by mine art)
Benighted in these woods! Now to my charms,   150
And to my wily trains: I shall ere long
Be well stock'd with as fair a herd as grazed
About my mother Circe. Thus I hurl

powdery My dazzling spells into the spongy air,
Of power to cheat the eye with blear illusion
And give it false presentments, lest the place
And my quaint habits breed astonishment,
And put the damsel to suspicious flight;
Which must not be, for that's against my course.
I under fair pretence of friendly ends   160
And well-placed words of glozing courtesy
Baited with reasons not unplausible,
Wind me into the easy-hearted man
And hug him into snares. When once her eye
Hath met the virtue of this magic dust,
I shall appear some harmless villager
Whom thrift keeps up about his country gear.
But here she comes; I fairly step aside
And hearken, if I may, her business here.

150 *Benighted*: overtaken by darkness.   151 *trains*: allurements or traps.
154 *spongy*: absorbent.   155 *Of power*: which (i.e. the spells) have the
power.   *blear*: dim, seen by a dazzled eye.   156 *false presentments*:
false images presented to the sight.   157 *quaint habits*: strange clothes.
See Nativity Ode, l. 194.   158 *suspicious flight*: flight caused by suspicion.   161 *glozing*: flattering.   163 *Wind me into*: insinuate
myself into favour with.   *easy-hearted*: unsuspecting.   164 *hug him
into*: draw him with kindness into.   165 *virtue*: efficacy (especially used
of medicinal herbs or preparations).   167 *gear*: occupation.
168 *fairly*: gently.

The Lady *enters.*

Lady. This way the noise was, if mine ear be true,   170
My best guide now. Methought it was the sound
Of riot and ill-managed merriment,
Such as the jocund flute or gamesome pipe
Stirs up among the loose unletter'd hinds,
When for their teeming flocks and granges full
In wanton dance they praise the bounteous Pan,
And thank the gods amiss. I should be loth
To meet the rudeness and swill'd insolence
Of such late wassailers; yet O where else
Shall I inform my unacquainted feet   180
In the blind mazes of this tangled wood?
My brothers when they saw me wearied out
With this long way, resolving here to lodge
Under the spreading favour of these pines,
Stepp'd, as they said, to the next thicket side
To bring me berries or such cooling fruit
As the kind hospitable woods provide.
They left me then when the gray-hooded Even
Like a sad votarist in palmer's weed
Rose from the hindmost wheels of Phoebus' wain.   190
But where they are, and why they came not back,

172 *ill-managed*: disorderly.   174 *loose*: wanton.   *unletter'd hinds*:
illiterate farm-workers.   175 *teeming*: multiplying. Cf. Nativity
Ode, l. 240.   *granges*: barns.   177 *amiss*: in a wrong manner.
178 *swill'd*: drunken.   179 *wassailers*: revellers. From *wassail*, 'good
health', a salutation used in drinking.   179–80 'Yet in what other
direction can I seek information to guide me on my path?'   181 *blind*:
dark.   183 *this long way*: this long journey.   184 *favour*: shelter.
185 *Stepp'd, as they said*: said they would walk a little way.   *next*: nearest.
189 *sad*: serious, staid. Cf. *Il Penseroso*, l. 43; *Lycidas*, l. 148.   *votarist*:
one who has taken a vow (here, to go on pilgrimage).   *palmer's weed*:
dress of a pilgrim.   190 *Phoebus wain*: the sun's chariot.

Is now the labour of my thoughts. 'Tis likeliest
They had engaged their wandering steps too far,
And envious darkness, ere they could return,
Had stole them from me: else O thievish Night,
Why shouldst thou, but for some felonious end,
In thy dark lantern thus close up the stars
That Nature hung in Heav'n, and fill'd their lamps
With everlasting oil, to give due light
To the misled and lonely traveller?   200
This is the place, as well as I may guess,
Whence even now the tumult of loud mirth
Was rife, and perfect in my listening ear,
Yet naught but single darkness do I find.
What might this be? A thousand fantasies
Begin to throng into my memory
Of calling shapes and beckoning shadows dire
And airy tongues that syllable men's names
On sands and shores and desert wildernesses.
These thoughts may startle well, but not astound   210
The virtuous mind, that ever walks attended
By a strong siding champion, Conscience.
O welcome, pure-eyed Faith, white-handed Hope,
Thou hovering angel girt with golden wings,
And thou unblemish'd form of Chastity!

193 *engaged*: committed (hence 'risked').   195 *else*: if it were not
so.   196 *felonious end*: criminal intent.   198 *and fill'd their lamps*:
'Filling their lamps' or 'whose lamps she filled' would be a more logical,
but less living, form of sentence. Cf. l. 6.   203 *rife*: flourishing.
perfect: complete; perhaps in the musical sense, of a sound that fills and
satisfies the ear.   204 *single darkness*: darkness alone.   205 *What
might this be?* 'What could be the meaning of this?'   208 *syllable*: call
out the syllables distinctly.   209 *desert*: uninhabited.   210 *may
startle well*: may indeed startle.   *astound*: strike with terror.
212 *siding*: supporting.   *Conscience*: pronounce 'Consci-ence'.
215 'And thou, Chastity, with unblemish'd (i.e. unspotted) form'.

I see ye visibly, and now believe
That he, the Supreme Good, t'whom all things ill
Are but as slavish officers of vengeance,
Would send a glistering guardian if need were
To keep my life and honour unassail'd.   220
Was I deceived, or did a sable cloud
Turn forth her silver lining on the night?
I did not err, there does a sable cloud
Turn forth her silver lining on the night,
And casts a gleam over this tufted grove.
I cannot hallo to my brothers, but
Such noise as I can make to be heard farthest
I'll venture, for my new-enliven'd spirits
Prompt me; and they perhaps are not far off.

SONG

Sweet Echo, sweetest Nymph that liv'st unseen   230
 Within thy airy shell
 By slow Meander's margent green,
And in the violet-embroider'd vale
 Where the love-lorn nightingale
Nightly to thee her sad song mourneth well:
Canst thou not tell me of a gentle pair
 That likest thy Narcissus are?
  O if thou have
 Hid them in some flowery cave,
 Tell me but where,   240

216 *visibly*: clearly.   218 *slavish officers of vengeance*: obedient instruments of God's vengeance.   221 *sable*: black.   226 *hallo*: call out loudly.   227 *to be heard farthest*: that may carry farthest.   228 *new-enliven'd*: newly encouraged.   232 *margent green*: either 'green margin' or 'green grass of the river's edge'.   235 *her sad song mourneth well*: 'laments beautifully in her song.'   236 *gentle*: noble.

Sweet Queen of Parley, daughter of the sphere!
So mayst thou be translated to the skies,
And give resounding grace to all Heav'n's harmonies.

Comus. Can any mortal mixture of Earth's mould
Breathe such divine enchanting ravishment?
Sure something holy lodges in that breast,
And with these raptures moves the vocal air
To testify his hidden residence.
How sweetly did they float upon the wings
Of silence, through the empty-vaulted night,   250
At every fall smoothing the raven down
Of darkness till it smiled! I have oft heard
My mother Circe with the Sirens three,
Amidst the flowery-kirtled Naiades
Culling their potent herbs and baleful drugs,
Who as they sung would take the prison'd soul
And lap it in Elysium; Scylla wept,
And chid her barking waves into attention,
And fell Charybdis murmur'd soft applause.
Yet they in pleasing slumber lull'd the sense,   260
And in sweet madness robb'd it of itself;
But such a sacred and home-felt delight,
Such sober certainty of waking bliss

241 *Parley*: colloquy.   242 *translated*: promoted.   *skies*: heaven.
243 *resounding grace*: the beauty of echoing sound.   244 *any . . . mould*:
'any human being, which must contain mixed elements and have an
earthly shape.'   246 *Sure*: surely.   247 *the vocal air*: the air which
carries the voice.   248 *his hidden residence*: the fact that it dwells there
unseen; 'his' is the old form of 'its'.   251 *fall*: musical cadence.   *raven*
down: black feathers.   252 *it*: i.e. darkness.   254 *flowery-kirtled*:
with gown or tunic woven of flowers.   255 *Culling*: gathering.
baleful: poisonous.   256 *take*: enrapture.   257 *lap*: enfold. See
L'Allegro, l. 136.   259 *fell*: wicked, destructive.   262 *home-felt*:
deeply felt, heart-felt.

I never heard till now. I'll speak to her,
And she shall be my queen. Hail, foreign wonder!
Whom certain these rough shades did never breed,
Unless the goddess that in rural shrine
Dwell'st here with Pan or Silvan, by blest song
Forbidding every bleak unkindly fog
To touch the prosperous growth of this tall wood.   270
Lady. Nay, gentle shepherd, ill is lost that praise
That is address'd to unattending ears.
Not any boast of skill, but extreme shift
How to regain my sever'd company
Compell'd me to awake the courteous Echo
To give me answer from her mossy couch.
Comus. What chance, good Lady, hath bereft you thus?
Lady. Dim darkness and this leavy labyrinth.
Comus. Could that divide you from near-ushering guides?
Lady. They left me weary on a grassy turf.   280
Comus. By falsehood, or discourtesy, or why?
Lady. To seek i' th' valley some cool friendly spring.
Comus. And left your fair side all unguarded, Lady?
Lady. They were but twain, and purposed quick return.
Comus. Perhaps forestalling night prevented them.
Lady. How easy my misfortune is to hit!
Comus. Imports their loss, beside the present need?
Lady. No less than if I should my brothers lose.
Comus. Were they of manly prime, or youthful bloom?

266 *rough shades*: wild forests.   267 *Unless the goddess*: 'unless you are the goddess.'   271 *ill is lost that praise*: 'that praise is sadly wasted.'   273 *boast of skill*: vain desire to display skill.   *extreme shift*: last resort.   274 *my sever'd company*: 'the companions from whom I have been parted.'   279 *near-ushering*: going ahead but keeping close.   285 *forestalling*: intervening.   286 *hit*: understand, perceive.   287 'Is your losing them important, apart from your present need of them (as guides)?'   288 'It is my brothers I have lost.'   289 *of manly prime*: in young manhood.   *youthful bloom*: adolescence.

Lady. As smooth as Hebe's their unrazor'd lips.   290
Comus. Two such I saw, what time the labour'd ox
In his loose traces from the furrow came
And the swink'd hedger at his supper sat.
I saw them under a green mantling vine
That crawls along the side of yon small hill,
Plucking ripe clusters from the tender shoots;
Their port was more than human, as they stood;
I took it for a faery vision
Of some gay creatures of the element
That in the colours of the rainbow live   300
And play i' th' plighted clouds. I was awe-strook,
And as I pass'd, I worshipp'd. If those you seek,
It were a journey like the path to Heaven
To help you find them.
Lady.   Gentle villager,
What readiest way would bring me to that place?
Comus. Due west it rises from this shrubby point.
Lady. To find out that, good shepherd, I suppose,
In such a scant allowance of star-light,
Would overtask the best land-pilot's art,
Without the sure guess of well-practised feet.   310
Comus. I know each lane and every alley green,
Dingle or bushy dell of this wild wood,
And every bosky bourn from side to side

290 *unrazor'd*: unshaven.   291 *what time*: when. Cf. *Lycidas*, l. 28.
labour'd: tired with work.   292 *In his loose traces*: with loosened
harness.   293 *swink'd*: tired out.   294 *mantling*: covering like a
mantle.   297 *port*: appearance, deportment.   298 *vision*: Pronounce 'visi-on'.   299 *element*: sky or air.   301 *plighted*: interwoven. Cf. 'tissued clouds', Nativity Ode, l. 146.   308 *scant allowance*:
small measure.   309 'Would be too hard a task for the skill of even
the best guide.'   310 The lack of starlight could only be compensated
by an intimate knowledge of the ground.   311 *lane*: a narrow by-way.
312 *Dingle*: valley-bottom.   313 *bosky bourn*: wooded stream.

COMUS 53

My daily walks and ancient neighbourhood;
And if your stray attendance be yet lodged
Or shroud within these limits, I shall know
Ere morrow wake or the low-roosted lark
From her thatch'd pallet rouse. If otherwise,
I can conduct you, Lady, to a low
But loyal cottage, where you may be safe   320
Till further quest.
Lady.   Shepherd, I take thy word
And trust thy honest offer'd courtesy,
Which oft is sooner found in lowly sheds
With smoky rafters, than in tap'stry halls
And courts of princes, where it first was named
And yet is most pretended. In a place
Less warranted than this or less secure
I cannot be, that I should fear to change it.
Eye me, blest Providence, and square my trial
To my proportion'd strength. Shepherd, lead on.   330

Enter the Two Brothers.

Elder Brother. Unmuffle, ye faint stars, and thou fair Moon
That wont'st to love the traveller's benison,
Stoop thy pale visage through an amber cloud

314 *ancient neighbourhood*: region I have lived in for many years.
315 *stray attendance*: attendants that have strayed.   316 *shroud*:
shelter, hide. See l. 147.   *limits*: boundaries.   318 *thatch'd*: grass-
covered.   *pallet*: straw mattress.   319 *low*: humble.   321 *quest*:
search.   322 *thy . . . courtesy*: the courtesy you offer me so honestly.
326 *And . . . pretended*: 'And is still most loudly claimed or professed'
(perhaps with the meaning also, that the 'pretension' is 'pretence').'
327 *warranted*: protected, safe.   328 *that*: so that.   329 *Eye me*:
keep me in your eye.   *square*: adjust, fit.   330 *proportion'd strength*:
strength allotted to me.   331 *Unmuffle*: take off your hood or veil.
332 *wont'st*: art accustomed to.   *benison*: blessing, thanks.   333 *Stoop*:
bend down. Cf. *Il Penseroso*, l. 71-2.

And disinherit Chaos, that reigns here
In double night of darkness and of shades;
Or if your influence be quite damm'd up
With black usurping mists, some gentle taper,
Though a rush candle from the wicker hole
Of some clay habitation, visit us
With thy long levell'd rule of streaming light,   340
And thou shalt be our star of Arcady
Or Tyrian Cynosure.
Second Brother.   Or if our eyes
Be barr'd that happiness, might we but hear
The folded flocks penn'd in their wattled cotes,
Or sound of pastoral reed with oaten stops,
Or whistle from the lodge, or village cock
Count the night watches to his feathery dames,
'Twould be some solace yet, some little cheering
In this close dungeon of innumerous boughs.
But O that hapless virgin, our lost sister!   350
Where may she wander now, whither betake her
From the chill dew, amongst rude burs and thistles?
Perhaps some cold bank is her bolster now
Or 'gainst the rugged bark of some broad elm
Leans her unpillow'd head, fraught with sad fears!

334 *disinherit*: displace.   335 *shades*: woods.   336 *influence*:
flowing light. Cf. Nativity Ode, l. 71.   337 *usurping*: taking over
the moon's realm.   *gentle*: kind, courteous.   338 *Though*: though
no better than.   *a rush candle*: a cheap candle made of a rush dipped in
tallow.   388–9 *wicker . . . habitation*: a hut made of osiers or wattle
covered with clay, of which the window would be only a hole.
340 *rule*: rod.   343 *barr'd*: refused.   *might . . . hear*: if only we could
hear.   344 *wattled cotes*: sheepfolds made of hurdles.   345 *pastoral
reed*: shepherd's pipe.   *oaten stops*: Cf. *Lycidas*, ll. 33, 88.   346 *lodge*:
small isolated house or hut.   347 *night watches*: night hours.   *dames*:
wives.   349 *innumerous*: innumerable.   351 *betake her*: remove
herself.

What if in wild amazement and affright,
Or while we speak, within the direful grasp
Of savage hunger or of savage heat?
Elder Brother. Peace, brother, be not over-exquisite
To cast the fashion of uncertain evils;   360
For grant they be so, while they rest unknown
What need a man forestall his date of grief
And run to meet what he would most avoid?
Or if they be but false alarms of fear,
How bitter is such self-delusion!
I do not think my sister so to seek,
Or so unprincipled in virtue's book
And the sweet peace that goodness bosoms ever,
As that the single want of light and noise
(Not being in danger, as I trust she is not)   370
Could stir the constant mood of her calm thoughts
And put them into misbecoming plight.
Virtue could see to do what virtue would
By her own radiant light, though sun and moon
Were in the flat sea sunk. And Wisdom's self
Oft seeks to sweet retirèd solitude,
Where with her best nurse Contemplation
She plumes her feathers and lets grow her wings,

356 *What if in*: 'What if she should be in.'   358 *heat*: lust.
359 *over-exquisite*: over-ingenious.   360 *cast the fashion*: forecast the
form.   *uncertain*: conjectural.   361 *grant they be so*: even if they
are as you imagine.   362 'Why need a man anticipate the time when he
will have to grieve?'   365 *delusion*: pronounce 'delusi-on'.   366 *so
to seek*: so much at a loss.   367 *unprincipled in virtue's book*: 'ungrounded
in the principles taught by virtue'.   368 *that goodness bosoms ever*: 'that
goodness always has in its heart'.   369 *single*: mere. Cf. l. 204.
370 'If she is not in danger, as I trust she is not.'   372 *misbecoming
plight*: distress that would be inappropriate.   373 *would*: would wish
to do.   375 *flat*: level.   *Wisdom's self*: Wisdom itself.   376 *seeks
to*: turns to.   377 *Contemplation*: pronounce 'Contemplati-on'. Cf.
Il Penseroso, l. 54.   378 *plumes*: preens.

That in the various bustle of resort
Were all-to ruffled and sometimes impair'd.   380
He that has light within his own clear breast
May sit i' the centre and enjoy bright day,
But he that hides a dark soul and foul thoughts
Benighted walks under the mid-day sun—
Himself is his own dungeon.
Second Brother.   'Tis most true
That musing meditation most affects
The pensive secrecy of desert cell,
Far from the cheerful haunt of men and herds,
And sits as safe as in a senate-house;
For who would rob a hermit of his weeds,   390
His few books or his beads or maple dish,
Or do his gray hairs any violence?
But beauty, like the fair Hesperian tree
Laden with blooming gold, had need the guard
Of dragon watch with unenchanted eye,
To save her blossoms and defend her fruit
From the rash hand of bold incontinence.
You may as well spread out the unsunn'd heaps
Of miser's treasure by an outlaw's den,
And tell me it is safe, as bid me hope   400
Danger will wink on opportunity
And let a single helpless maiden pass

379 *various bustle of resort*: the variety and business of crowds.
380 *all-to*: extremely.   *impair'd*: damaged.   381 *clear*: noble and
open. Cf. *Lycidas*, l. 70.   382 *the centre*: i.e. the centre of the earth.
383 *hides*: harbours.   384 *Benighted*: sunk in darkness. Cf. l. 150.
386 *most affects*: is most inclined to, prefers.   388 *haunt of*: place
frequented by.   390 *weeds*: clothes. Cf. ll. 16, 84.   391 *beads*:
rosary.   394 *had need the guard*: would need the protection.
395 *dragon watch*: watch kept by a dragon.   *unenchanted*: not to be
enchanted. Cf. 'uncontrollèd', l. 793.   398 *unsunn'd*: kept in the dark,
hidden.   401 *Danger*: power to harm.   *wink on*: refuse to see.

Uninjured in this wild surrounding waste.
Of night or loneliness it recks me not;
I fear the dread events that dog them both,
Lest some ill-greeting touch attempt the person
Of our unownèd sister.
Elder Brother.   I do not, brother,
Infer as if I thought my sister's state
Secure without all doubt or controversy;
Yet where an equal poise of hope and fear   410
Does arbitrate th' event, my nature is
That I incline to hope rather than fear,
And gladly banish squint suspicion.
My sister is not so defenceless left
As you imagine; she has a hidden strength
Which you remember not.
Second Brother.   What hidden strength,
Unless the strength of Heav'n, if you mean that?
Elder Brother. I mean that too, but yet a hidden strength
Which if Heav'n gave it, may be term'd her own;
'Tis chastity, my brother, chastity: 420
She that has that, is clad in complete steel,
And like a quiver'd nymph with arrows keen
May trace huge forests and unharbour'd heaths,
Infamous hills and sandy perilous wilds,
Where through the sacred rays of chastity,
No savage fierce, bandit or mountaineer

404 *it recks me not*: I take no account. Cf. *Lycidas*, l. 122.   406 *ill-greeting*: discourteous.   407 *unownèd*: unprotected.   408 *Infer*: argue, reason.   410 *poise*: balance.   411 *arbitrate th' event*: debate what may be the outcome.   413 *squint suspicion*: suspiciousness looking askance (at what may happen).   419 *if*: even if.   421 *complete steel*: full armour.   422 *quiver'd*: carrying a quiver.   423 *trace*: track, tread through.   *unharbour'd*: shelterless.   424 *Infamous*: of bad reputation, dangerous.   425 *through*: because of.   426 *mountaineer*: mountain-dweller (meaning 'a wild savage').

Will dare to soil her virgin purity;
Yea, there where very desolation dwells,
By grots and caverns shagg'd with horrid shades,
She may pass on with unblench'd majesty,   430
Be it not done in pride or in presumption.
Some say no evil thing that walks by night
In fog or fire, by lake or moorish fen,
Blue meagre hag, or stubborn unlaid ghost
That breaks his magic chains at curfew time,
No goblin or swart faery of the mine,
Hath hurtful power o'er true virginity.
Do ye believe me yet, or shall I call
Antiquity from the old schools of Greece
To testify the arms of chastity?   440
Hence had the huntress Dian her dread bow,
Fair silver-shafted queen for ever chaste,
Wherewith she tamed the brinded lioness
And spotted mountain pard, but set at nought
The frivolous bolt of Cupid; gods and men
Fear'd her stern frown, and she was queen o' th' woods.
What was that snaky-headed Gorgon shield
That wise Minerva wore, unconquer'd virgin,
Wherewith she freezed her foes to congeal'd stone,
But rigid looks of chaste austerity,   450
And noble grace that dash'd brute violence

429 *shagg'd*: overgrown. *horrid shades*: bristling woods.   430 *un-blench'd*: unstartled.   431 'If she does not act through pride or presumptuousness.'   433 *moorish*: heathy.   434 *Blue*: pale, livid. *meagre*: skinny.   *hag*: an evil spirit (also a witch).   *unlaid*: refusing to be exorcized.   435 *curfew time*: lights out.   436 *swart*: swarthy. 438 *Do ye believe me yet*: 'Have I convinced you yet?'   439 *schools*: schools of philosophy.   440 *arms*: weapons.   442 *silver-shafted*: armed with silver arrows.   443 *brinded*: brindled.   444 *pard*: leopard.   445 *bolt*: arrow.   449 *congeal'd*: accent 'cóngeal'd'. 450 *rigid*: stern, unchanging.

With sudden adoration and blank awe?
So dear to Heav'n is saintly chastity
That when a soul is found sincerely so
A thousand liveried angels lackey her,
Driving far off each thing of sin and guilt,
And in clear dream and solemn vision
Tell her of things that no gross ear can hear,
Till oft converse with heavenly habitants
Begin to cast a beam on th' outward shape,   460
The unpolluted temple of the mind,
And turns it by degrees to the soul's essence,
Till all be made immortal. But when lust
By unchaste looks, loose gestures and foul talk,
But most by lewd and lavish act of sin,
Lets in defilement to the inward parts,
The soul grows clotted by contagion,
Imbodies and imbrutes, till she quite lose
The divine property of her first being.
Such are those thick and gloomy shadows damp   470
Oft seen in charnel vaults and sepulchres
Lingering, and sitting by a new-made grave,
As loth to leave the body that it loved,
And link'd itself by carnal sensualty

452 *blank awe*: helpless amazement and fear.   454 *sincerely so*: wholly chaste. Cf. *On Time*, l. 14.   455 *liveried*: wearing garments showing that they are servants (of God).   457 *clear*: explicit.   *vision*: pronounce 'visi-on.'   458 *gross*: ignorant, crude.   459 *oft converse*: frequent conversation.   461 *temple of the mind*: i.e. the body. 465 *lewd*: base, lustful.   *lavish*: unrestrained.   467 *clotted*: thickened, coarsened.   *contagion*: pronounce 'contagi-on'.   468 *Imbodies and imbrutes*: becomes materialized and brutish.   469 *divine*: accent 'divine'.   *property*: essential quality.   *first being*: original state of being. 471 *charnel-vaults*: burial vaults.   473 *As loth*: 'as if it (such a soul) were unwilling'.   474 *And link'd itself*: and so linked itself.   *sensualty*: sensuality, subjection to the senses.

To a degenerate and degraded state.
Second Brother. How charming is divine philosophy!
Not harsh and crabbèd, as dull fools suppose,
But musical as in Apollo's lute,
And a perpetual feast of nectar'd sweets
Where no crude surfeit reigns.
Elder Brother.   List, list, I hear   480
Some far-off hallo break the silent air.
Second Brother. Methought so too; what should it be?
Elder Brother.   For certain
Either some one like us night-founder'd here,
Or else some neighbour woodman, or at worst
Some roving robber calling to his fellows.
Second Brother. Heaven keep my sister! Again, again, and
      near?
Best draw, and stand upon our guard.
Elder Brother.   I'll hallo.
If he be friendly he comes well; if not,
Defence is a good cause, and Heaven be for us.

> *He hallos. There is an answering hallo, and the*
> Attendant Spirit *enters, habited like a shepherd.*

Elder Brother. That hallo I should know. What are you?
      speak:
Come not too near, you fall on iron stakes else.   491
Spirit. What voice is that? my young Lord? speak again.
Second Brother. O brother, 'tis my father's shepherd, sure.
Elder Brother. Thyrsis! whose artful strains have oft delay'd

---

   477 *crabbèd*: ill tempered.   479 *nectar'd*: richly flavoured.
480 *crude surfeit*: overeating bringing indigestion.   *reigns*: prevails.
List: hark.   481 *hallo*: loud call. See l. 226.   483 *night-founder'd*:
lost at night.   487 *Best draw*: 'We had better draw our swords.'
488 *he comes well*: he is welcome.   (Stage Direction) *habited*: dressed.
490 *I should know*: I think I know.   494 *artful strains*: skilful music.

The huddling brook to hear his madrigal,
And sweeten'd every musk-rose of the dale.
How camest thou here, good swain? hath any ram
Slipp'd from the fold, or young kid lost his dam,
Or straggling wether the pent flock forsook?
How couldst thou find this dark sequester'd nook?   500
Spirit. O my loved master's heir, and his next joy,
I came not here on such a trivial toy
As a stray'd ewe, or to pursue the stealth
Of pilfering wolf: not all the fleecy wealth
That doth enrich these downs is worth a thought
To this my errand, and the care it brought.
But O my virgin Lady, where is she?
How chance she is not in your company?
Elder Brother. To tell thee sadly, shepherd, without blame
Or our neglect, we lost her as we came.   510
Spirit. Ay me unhappy! then my fears are true.
Elder Brother. What fears, good Thyrsis? prithee briefly
    shew.
Spirit. I'll tell ye. 'Tis not vain or fabulous
(Though so esteem'd by shallow ignorance)
What the sage poets, taught by th' heavenly Muse,
Storied of old in high immortal verse
Of dire Chimeras and enchanted isles,
And rifted rocks whose entrance leads to Hell;
For such there be, but unbelief is blind.

---

495 *huddling*: tumbling.   499 *straggling*: straying.   *wether*:
castrated ram.   *pent*: penned in the fold.   501 'His next joy'
refers to the younger brother, next in age, and also the joy of his father.
502 *toy*: trifling object.   506 *To*: compared to.   508 *How chance*:
'how does it happen that.'   509 *sadly*: seriously. See l. 189.
512 *shew*: show. Pronounce to rhyme with 'true'.   513 *fabulous*:
merely legendary.   516 *Storied*: related.   518 *rifted*:
split.

Within the navel of this hideous wood,   520
Immured in cypress shades a sorcerer dwells,
Of Bacchus and of Circe born, great Comus,
Deep skill'd in all his mother's witcheries;
And here to every thirsty wanderer
By sly enticement gives his baneful cup
With many murmurs mix'd, whose pleasing poison
The visage quite transforms of him that drinks,
And the inglorious likeness of a beast
Fixes instead, unmoulding reason's mintage
Character'd in the face. This have I learnt   530
Tending my flocks hard by i' th' hilly crofts
That brow this bottom glade, whence night by night
He and his monstrous rout are heard to howl
Like stabled wolves, or tigers at their prey,
Doing abhorrèd rites to Hecate
In their obscurèd haunts of inmost bowers;
Yet have they many baits and guileful spells
To inveigle and invite the unwary sense
Of them that pass unweeting by the way.
This evening late (by then the chewing flocks   540
Had ta'en their supper on the savoury herb
Of knot-grass dew-besprent, and were in fold)
I sate me down to watch upon a bank
With ivy canopied and interwove

520 *navel*: centre.   521 *Immured in*: walled in by.   526 *murmurs*:
murmured spells.   529 *unmoulding . . . mintage*: destroying the form
stamped by reason (i.e. by the soul).   530 *Character'd*: written.
531 *crofts*: fields.   532 *brow*: overhang.   *bottom glade*: glade in the
valley bottom.   533 *monstrous rout*: crew of monsters. Cf. *Lycidas*,
l. 158.   534 *stabled wolves*: wolves that have entered a sheepfold.
535 *abhorrèd rites*: disgusting religious ceremonies.   *to*: in honour of.
538 *unwary sense*: reason which is not on the watch.   539 *unweeting*:
in ignorance (unwitting).   540 *by then*: by the time that.   542 *be-
sprent*: besprinkled.

With flaunting honeysuckle, and began,
Wrapt in a fit of pleasing melancholy,
To meditate my rural minstrelsy
Till fancy had her fill; but ere a close
The wonted roar was up amidst the woods
And fill'd the air with barbarous dissonance: 550
At which I ceased, and listen'd them a while
Till an unusual stop of sudden silence
Gave respite to the drowsy-frighted steeds
That draw the litter of close-curtain'd sleep.
At last a soft and solemn-breathing sound
Rose like a stream of rich distill'd perfumes
And stole upon the air, that even Silence
Was took ere she was ware and wish'd she might
Deny her nature and be never more,
Still to be so displaced. I was all ear,   560
And took in strains that might create a soul
Under the ribs of Death. But O ere long
Too well I did perceive it was the voice
Of my most honour'd Lady, your dear sister:
Amazed I stood, harrow'd with grief and fear,
And 'O poor hapless nightingale,' thought I,
'How sweet thou sing'st, how near the deadly snare!'
Then down the lawns I ran with headlong haste
Through paths and turnings often trod by day,
Till guided by mine ear I found the place   570

545 *flaunting*: waving its flowers.   546 *Wrapt*: engrossed. Cf.
Nativity Ode, l. 134.   *melancholy*: thoughtfulness. See *Il Penseroso*.
547 *meditate*: study.   548 *fancy*: poetic or creative imagination.   *ere*
a close: before I came to a cadence (in the song).   549 *was up*:
set up.   553 *drowsy-frighted*: drowsy but frightened off (by the uproar).
554 *litter*: couch in the form of a vehicle.   558 *took*: charmed, en-
snared. Cf. l. 256.   560 *Still . . . displaced*: 'If only she might always
be displaced by such music.'   561 *strains*: cf. l. 494.   565 *harrow'd*:
torn.   568 *lawns*: grassy spaces between trees. See Nativity Ode, l. 85.

Where that damn'd wizard, hid in sly disguise
(For so by certain signs I knew) had met
Already, ere my best speed could prevent,
The aidless innocent Lady, his wish'd prey;
Who gently ask'd if he had seen such two,
Supposing him some neighbour villager.
Longer I durst not stay, but soon I guess'd
Ye were the two she meant; with that I sprung
Into swift flight, till I had found you here;
But further know I not.

Second Brother.   O night and shades,   580
How are ye join'd with hell in triple knot
Against th' unarmèd weakness of one virgin,
Alone and helpless! Is this the confidence
You gave me, brother?

Elder Brother.   Yes, and keep it still,
Lean on it safely; not a period
Shall be unsaid for me. Against the threats
Of malice or of sorcery, or that power
Which erring men call Chance, this I hold firm:
Virtue may be assail'd, but never hurt,
Surprised by unjust force, but not enthrall'd;   590
Yea, even that which mischief meant most harm
Shall in the happy trial prove most glory.
But evil on itself shall back recoil
And mix no more with goodness, when at last
Gather'd like scum and settled to itself,

---

574 *aidless*: helpless. *his wish'd prey*: the prey he desired.   575 *such
two*: a certain couple.   580 *shades*: woods.   583 *confidence*: assurance.   585 *Lean*: rely.   *period*: sentence.   586 *for me*: for
my part.   590 *enthrall'd*: enslaved.   591 *mischief meant most harm*:
malice meant to be most harmful.   592 *happy trial*: test with a happy
outcome.   594 *at last*: i.e. at the end of time, in the Last Judgment.
595 *settled to itself*: settling into itself (like dregs).

It shall be in eternal restless change
Self-fed and self-consumed: if this fail,
The pillar'd firmament is rottenness
And earth's base built on stubble. But come, let's on!
Against the opposing will and arm of Heaven   600
May never this just sword be lifted up:
But for that damn'd magician, let him be girt
With all the grisly legions that troop
Under the sooty flag of Acheron,
Harpies and Hydras, or all the monstrous forms
'Twixt Africa and Inde, I'll find him out
And force him to restore his purchase back,
Or drag him by the curls to a foul death
Cursed as his life.
Spirit.   Alas good vent'rous youth,
I love thy courage yet, and bold emprise,   610
But here thy sword can do thee little stead;
Far other arms and other weapons must
Be those that quell the might of hellish charms:
He with his bare wand can unthread thy joints
And crumble all thy sinews.
Elder Brother.   Why, prithee Shepherd,
How durst thou then thyself approach so near
As to make this relation?
Spirit.   Care and utmost shifts
How to secure the Lady from surprisal

---

598 *firmament*: sky. 602 *But for*: but as for. 603 *legions*: pronounce 'legi-ons'. *troop*: assemble as an army. 606 *Inde*: India (from Old French *Ynde*, Persian *Hind*). 607 *purchase*: booty, something obtained by theft. 608 *foul*: dishonourable. 609 *vent'rous*: brave. 610 *yet*: though it is useless. *emprise*: enterprise. 611 *stead*: service. 614 *bare wand*: mere wand. *unthread*: loosen, dissolve. 615 *prithee*: pray tell me. 617 *relation*: report (of what he heard). *utmost shifts*: last resort; see l. 273.

Brought to my mind a certain shepherd lad,
Of small regard to see to, yet well skill'd   620
In every virtuous plant and healing herb
That spreads her verdant leaf to the morning ray.
He loved me well, and oft would beg me sing;
Which when I did, he on the tender grass
Would sit and hearken even to ecstasy,
And in requital ope his leathern scrip
And shew me simples of a thousand names,
Telling their strange and vigorous faculties.
Amongst the rest a small unsightly root,
But of divine effect, he cull'd me out;   630
The leaf was darkish, and had prickles on it,
But in another country, as he said,
Bore a bright golden flower, but not in this soil:
Unknown, and like esteem'd, and the dull swain
Treads on it daily with his clouted shoon;
And yet more med'cinal is it than that Moly
That Hermes once to wise Ulysses gave.
He call'd it Haemony, and gave it me,
And bade me keep it as of sovran use
'Gainst all enchantments, mildew blast or damp   640
Or ghastly Furies' apparition.

620 *small regard*: little account.   *to see to*: to look at.   *well skill'd*:
deeply learned.   621 *virtuous*: having medicinal properties. See l. 165.
624 *tender*: young, fresh.   625 *even to ecstasy*: until he was in rapture.
626 *in requital*: as a recompense.   *scrip*: pouch.   627 *simples*: medicinal
herbs ('simple' because not compounded to make medicines).   630 *divine
effect*: supernatural power to do good.   *cull'd*: picked, chose. See l. 255.
me: for me.   633 Accent 'in thís soil'.   634 *like esteem'd*: valued as
little (as known).   *swain*: countryman. See l. 84.   635 *clouted shoon*:
shoes either patched or studded with nails.   636 Accent 'mèd'cinal'.
that: that famous (Lat. *ille*).   639 *sovran*: sovereign (but with additional
sense of 'remedial'). See l. 41.   640 *mildew blast*: blighting mildew
(infection of plants or animals attributed to evil spirits).   *damp*: noxious
gas or vapour.   641 *apparition*: pronounce 'appariti-on'.

I pursed it up, but little reckoning made
Till now that this extremity compell'd,
But now I find it true; for by this means
I knew the foul enchanter though disguised,
Enter'd the very lime-twigs of his spells
And yet came off. If you have this about you
(As I will give you when we go) you may
Boldly assault the necromancer's hall:
Where if he be, with dauntless hardihood   650
And brandish'd blade rush on him, break his glass
And shed the luscious liquor on the ground.
But seize his wand; though he and his curst crew
Fierce sign of battle make, and menace high,
Or like the sons of Vulcan vomit smoke,
Yet will they soon retire, if he but shrink.
Elder Brother. Thyrsis, lead on apace, I'll follow thee;
And some good angel bear a shield before us.

*The Scene changes to a stately palace, set out with all manner of
deliciousness; soft music, tables spread with all dainties.* Comus
appears with his rabble, and the Lady *set in an enchanted chair;
to whom he offers his glass, which she puts by, and goes about
to rise.*

Comus. Nay, Lady, sit; if I but wave this wand,
Your nerves are all chain'd up in alabaster,   660

642 *pursed it up*: put it in my purse.   *little reckoning made*: thought
little about it.   643 *extremity*: extreme necessity.   646 *lime-twigs*:
snares for birds, made of twigs smeared with sticky substance (birdlime).
647 *came off*: escaped.   648 *As I will give you*: 'And for this purpose I will give it you.'   649 *hall*: palace. See l. 835.   650 *hardihood*: courage.   652 *luscious*: richly flavoured.   653 *curst*: evil.
crew: crowd of followers.   654 *menace high*: great threats.
(Stage Direction) *set in*: seated in.   *puts by*: refuses.   *goes about*: attempts.   660 *nerves*: sinews.   *alabaster*: a stone often used for monumental statues.

And you a statue, or as Daphne was
Root-bound, that fled Apollo.
Lady.   Fool, do not boast:
Thou canst not touch the freedom of my mind
With all thy charms, although this corporal rind
Thou hast immanacled, while Heaven sees good.
Comus. Why are you vex'd, Lady? why do you frown?
Here dwell no frowns nor anger, from these gates
Sorrow flies far. See here be all the pleasures
That fancy can beget on youthful thoughts,
When the fresh blood grows lively and returns   670
Brisk as the April buds in primrose-season.
And first behold this cordial julep here
That flames and dances in his crystal bounds,
With spirits of balm, and fragrant syrups mix'd;
Not that Nepenthes which the wife of Thonè
In Egypt gave to Jove-born Helena
Is of such power to stir up joy as this,
To life so friendly or so cool to thirst.
Why should you be so cruel to yourself,
And to those dainty limbs which Nature lent   680
For gentle usage and soft delicacy?
But you invert the covenants of her trust,
And harshly deal like an ill borrower
With that which you received on other terms,

662 *Root-bound*: fixed by a root (cf. the expression 'rooted to the
spot').   664 *corporal rind*: the case of the body.   665 *immanacled*:
fettered.   *while*: for as long as.   669 *fancy*: amorous desire.
670 *returns*: revives.   672 *cordial*: invigorating.   *julep*: a sweet drink.
673 *flames*: shines.   *his*: its.   *crystal bounds*: the glass goblet holding
it.   675 Pronounce 'Nepenthès'.   680 *dainty*: graceful, attractive.
lent: gave, but only for a time.   682 'But you reverse the conditions
on which she (Nature) agreed to lend.'   684 *on other terms*:
i.e. on generous terms.

Scorning the unexempt condition
By which all mortal frailty must subsist,
Refreshment after toil, ease after pain,
That have been tired all day without repast
And timely rest have wanted. But, fair virgin,
This will restore all soon.

Lady.   'Twill not, false traitor;   690
'Twill not restore the truth and honesty
That thou hast banish'd from thy tongue with lies.
Was this the cottage and the safe abode
Thou told'st me of? What grim aspects are these,
These ugly-headed monsters? Mercy guard me!
Hence with thy brew'd enchantments, foul deceiver:
Hast thou betray'd my credulous innocence
With visor'd falsehood and base forgery,
And wouldst thou seek again to trap me here
With lickerish baits fit to ensnare a brute?   700
Were it a draught for Juno when she banquets,
I would not taste thy treasonous offer; none
But such as are good men can give good things,
And that which is not good is not delicious
To a well-govern'd and wise appetite.

Comus. O foolishness of men! that lend their ears
To those budge doctors of the Stoic fur,
And fetch their precepts from the Cynic tub,
Praising the lean and sallow Abstinence.

685 *unexempt condition*: condition from which no one is exempted.
Pronounce 'conditi-on'.   686 *all mortal frailty*: the weakness of all
living creatures.   688 *That*: refers to 'you', l. 682.   689 *wanted*:
gone without.   694 *aspects*: looks. Accent 'aspècts'.   696 *brew'd
enchantments*: magic potions.   698 *visor'd*: masked. *forgery*: deception.   700 *lickerish*: appetizing.   701 *draught for*: drink fit for.
705 *well-govern'd*: controlled by virtue.   707 *budge doctors*: pom-
pous teachers. 'Budge' was a kind of lambskin fur used to trim university
or other gowns.   708 *fetch*: draw.

Wherefore did Nature pour her bounties forth   710
With such a full and unwithdrawing hand,
Covering the earth with odours, fruits and flocks,
Thronging the seas with spawn innumerable,
But all to please and sate the curious taste?
And set to work millions of spinning worms
That in their green shops weave the smooth-hair'd silk,
To deck her sons; and that no corner might
Be vacant of her plenty, in her own loins
She hutch'd th' all-worshipp'd ore and precious gems,
To store her children with. If all the world   720
Should in a pet of temperance feed on pulse,
Drink the clear stream and nothing wear but frieze,
Th' All-Giver would be unthank'd, would be unpraised,
Not half his riches known, and yet despised;
And we should serve him as a grudging master,
As a penurious niggard of his wealth,
And live like Nature's bastards, not her sons:
Who would be quite surcharged with her own weight
And strangled with her waste fertility;
Th' earth cumber'd, and the wing'd air dark'd with
     plumes,   730
The herds would over-multitude their lords,

711 *unwithdrawing*: unstinting.   712 *odours*: scented flowers.
714 *sate*: satisfy. *curious*: critical.   716 *green shops*: enclosures of
leaves.   718 *her own loins*: Nature's body, the earth.   719 *hutch'd*:
shut up in a chest, coffered. *all-worshipp'd*: universally prized.   720 *To
store her children with*: to provide for her children.   721 *pet*: fit of
temper. *pulse*: peas and beans, i.e. simple food.   722 *frieze*:
cheap woollen cloth.   723 *Th' All-Giver*: God, who gives Nature,
which gives abundance.   724 'Less than half his riches being known,
and even that despised.'   725 *as . . . master*: as if he were a mean
employer.   727 'And live as if we were not (as we are) legitimate
heirs to the wealth of Nature.'   728 *Who*: i.e. Nature. *surcharged*:
overloaded.   729 *strangled*: stifled.   730 *wing'd*: supporting
wings.   731 *over-multitude*: outnumber. *their lords*: i.e. men

The sea o'erfraught would swell, and th' unsought diamonds
Would so emblaze the forehead of the deep
And so bestud with stars, that they below
Would grow inured to light, and come at last
To gaze upon the sun with shameless brows.
List Lady, be not coy and be not cozen'd
With that same vaunted name, Virginity:
Beauty is Nature's coin, must not be hoarded,
But must be current, and the good thereof   740
Consists in mutual and partaken bliss,
Unsavoury in th' enjoyment of itself;
If you let slip time, like a neglected rose
It withers on the stalk with languish'd head.
Beauty is Nature's brag, and must be shown
In courts, at feasts and high solemnities
Where most may wonder at the workmanship.
It is for homely features to keep home,
They had their name thence; coarse complexions
And cheeks of sorry grain will serve to ply   750
The sampler and to tease the huswife's wool:
What need a vermeil-tinctured lip for that,
Love-darting eyes or tresses like the morn?

732 *o'erfraught*: overfull (of fish). Cf. l. 355.   733 *emblaze*: light up.
deep: depth or centre of the earth.   734 *they below*: dwellers underground (i.e. spirits or ghosts of the underworld).   735 *inured*:
accustomed.   *at last*: eventually.   737 *cozen'd*: deceived.
738 *that . . . name*: 'that mere word or title which is so often boasted of.'
739 *coin*: currency.   740 *current*: circulating, in use.   *good*: benefit.
741 *partaken*: shared out.   742 *Unsavoury*: insipid.   *enjoyment of itself*: i.e. Beauty's.   743 Scan: 'If you lét slíp tíme, líke a neglécted
róse.'   745 *brag*: pomp and display.   746 *solemnities*: festivals.
Cf. l. 142.   748 *homely*: plain.   *keep home*: stay at home.
749 Pronounce 'complexi-ons'.   750 *sorry grain*: poor colour. See *Il
Penseroso*, l. 33.   *ply*: work busily at.   751 *sampler*: specimen of
needlework.   *tease*: comb, untangle.   *huswife's*: pronounce 'hussif's'.
752 *vermeil-tinctured*: tinted with vermilion.

There was another meaning in these gifts:
Think what, and be advised; you are but young yet.
Lady. I had not thought to have unlock'd my lips
In this unhallow'd air, but that this juggler
Would think to charm my judgment, as mine eyes,
Obtruding false rules prank'd in reason's garb.
I hate when vice can bolt her arguments   760
And virtue has no tongue to check her pride.
Impostor! do not charge most innocent Nature,
As if she would her children should be riotous
With her abundance. She, good cateress,
Means her provision only to the good,
That live according to her sober laws
And holy dictate of spare Temperance.
If every just man that now pines with want
Had but a moderate and beseeming share
Of that which lewdly-pamper'd Luxury   770
Now heaps upon some few with vast excess,
Nature's full blessings would be well dispensed
In unsuperfluous even proportion,
And she no whit encumber'd with her store.
And then the Giver would be better thank'd,
His praise due paid; for swinish gluttony
Ne'er looks to Heaven amidst his gorgeous feast,
But with besotted base ingratitude

755 *Think what*: consider what it might be.   *be advised*: come to a
sound conclusion.   757 *juggler*: magician.   758 *as mine eyes*: as
he did my eyes. See ll. 153–67.   759 *Obtruding*: putting forward.
prank'd: decked out.   760 *I hate*: I am indignant.   *bolt*: shoot out
(from 'bolt', an arrow).   763 *riotous*: extravagant.   764 *cateress*:
provider of material goods.   765 *Means*: intends.   767 *spare*: frugal.
Cf. *Il Penseroso*, l. 46.   768 *pines*: starves, wastes away.   769 *beseeming*: appropriate.   770 *lewdly-pamper'd*: grossly overfed.   772 *dispensed*:
shared out.   774 *store*: abundance.   777 *gorgeous*: magnificent (but
associated with gluttony).   778 *besotted*: stupefied.   *base*: low-minded.

Crams, and blasphemes his feeder. Shall I go on?
Or have I said enough? To him that dares   780
Arm his profane tongue with contemptuous words
Against the sun-clad power of Chastity,
Fain would I something say; yet to what end?
Thou hast nor ear nor soul to apprehend
The sublime notion and high mystery,
That must be utter'd to unfold the sage
And serious doctrine of Virginity;
And thou art worthy that thou shouldst not know
More happiness than this thy present lot.
Enjoy your dear wit and gay rhetoric,   790
That hath so well been taught her dazzling fence:
Thou art not fit to hear thyself convinced.
Yet should I try, the uncontrollèd worth
Of this pure cause would kindle my rapt spirits
To such a flame of sacred vehemence
That dumb things would be moved to sympathise,
And the brute Earth would lend her nerves, and shake
Till all thy magic structures, rear'd so high,
Were shatter'd into heaps o'er thy false head.
Comus. She fables not. I feel that I do fear   800
Her words set off by some superior power;
And though not mortal, yet a cold shuddering dew
Dips me all o'er, as when the wrath of Jove

779 *Crams*: stuffs himself.   *blasphemes*: insults (by his greed).   783
Fain: willingly.   786 *utter'd*: set out.   *unfold*: expound.   788 'And
you are unworthy to know.'   790 *dear wit*: the cleverness you delight in.   *gay*: smart.   791 *fence*: fencing with words, verbal skill.
793 *uncontrollèd*: irrepressible.   794 *rapt*: ecstatic. Cf. l. 546.
797 *brute*: senseless.   *lend*: assist with.   *nerves*: sinews. Cf. l. 660.
800 *fables not*: is not inventing stories.   801 *set off*: backed up.
802 *And ... mortal*: and though I am immortal.   *shuddering*: making
shudder.   803 *Dips*: bathes.

Speaks thunder and the chains of Erebus
To some of Saturn's crew. I must dissemble,
And try her yet more strongly. Come, no more!
This is mere moral babble, and direct
Against the canon laws of our foundation:
I must not suffer this; yet 'tis but the lees
And settlings of a melancholy blood.   810
But this will cure all straight; one sip of this
Will bathe the drooping spirits in delight
Beyond the bliss of dreams. Be wise, and taste.—

The Brothers *rush in with swords drawn, wrest his glass out of his hand, and break it against the ground; his rout make sign of resistance, but are all driven in. The* Attendant Spirit *comes in.*

Spirit. What, have you let the false enchanter 'scape?
O ye mistook, ye should have snatch'd his wand
And bound him fast; without his rod reversed,
And backward mutters of dissevering power,
We cannot free the Lady that sits here
In stony fetters fix'd and motionless.
Yet stay, be not disturb'd; now I bethink me,   820
Some other means I have which may be used,
Which once of Meliboeus old I learnt,
The soothest shepherd that ere piped on plains.
     There is a gentle Nymph not far from hence,

804 *Speaks*: both 'utters (thunder)' and 'pronounces sentence of (chains)'.
805 *crew*: followers.   807 *mere moral babble*: nothing but pious verbiage.
808 *canon laws . . . foundation*: constitutional laws of our society (as founded
for pleasure).   809–10 *lees And settlings*: dregs and sediments.
811 *straight:* at once. See *L'Allegro*, l. 69.   812 *drooping*: sinking.
816–17 'Without holding his rod upside down and saying his spells back-
wards so as to dissolve their effect.'   *mutters*: muttered spells.   *dissevering*: unbinding.   823 *soothest*: most truthful.

That with moist curb sways the smooth Severn stream:
Sabrina is her name, a virgin pure;
Whilom she was the daughter of Locrine,
That had the sceptre from his father Brute.
The guiltless damsel flying the mad pursuit
Of her enragèd stepdam, Guendolen,   830
Commended her fair innocence to the flood
That stay'd her flight with his cross-flowing course:
The water-nymphs that in the bottom play'd
Held up their pearlèd wrists and took her in,
Bearing her straight to agèd Nereus' hall,
Who piteous of her woes, rear'd her lank head,
And gave her to his daughters to imbathe
In nectar'd lavers strew'd with asphodel;
And through the porch and inlet of each sense
Dropp'd in ambrosial oils till she revived   840
And underwent a quick immortal change,
Made goddess of the river. Still she retains
Her maiden gentleness, and oft at eve
Visits the herds along the twilight meadows,
Helping all urchin blasts and ill-luck signs
That the shrewd meddling elf delights to make,
Which she with precious viall'd liquors heals:
For which the shepherds at their festivals

825 *moist curb*: authority of a river goddess.   *sways*: governs. Cf. l. 18.
827 *Whilom*: formerly.   828 *had the sceptre*: inherited the kingdom.
830 *stepdam*: stepmother.   831 *Commended*: entrusted.   *flood*: river.
835 *straight*: see l. 811.   *hall*: see l. 649.   836 *rear'd*: raised. See l. 798.
lank: drooping or wet.   837 *imbathe*: bathe thoroughly.   838 *nectar'd*
lavers: baths or bowls sweetly perfumed. See l. 479, and *Lycidas*, l. 175.
839 *porch and inlet*: entrance and opening.   840 *ambrosial*: heavenly.
Cf. l. 16.   841 *immortal change*: change to an immortal. 'Quick'
means 'living' as well as 'rapid'.   843 *gentleness*: kindness.   845 *Help-*
ing: remedying.   *urchin blasts*: evil blights; see l. 640.   746 *shrewd*:
spiteful.   847 *viall'd*: stored in vials (glass vessels).

Carol her goodness loud in rustic lays,
And throw sweet garland wreaths into her stream   850
Of pansies, pinks and gaudy daffodils.
And as the old swain said, she can unlock
The clasping charm and thaw the numbing spell,
If she be right invoked in warbled song;
For maidenhood she loves, and will be swift
To aid a virgin, such as was herself,
In hard-besetting need. This will I try,
And add the power of some adjuring verse.

SONG

Sabrina fair
  Listen where thou art sitting   860
Under the glassy, cool, translucent wave,
  In twisted braids of lilies knitting
The loose train of thy amber-dropping hair;
  Listen for dear honour's sake,
  Goddess of the silver lake,
    Listen and save!

Listen, and appear to us
In name of great Oceanus,
By the earth-shaking Neptune's mace,
And Tethys' grave majestic pace,   870
By hoary Nereus' wrinkled look,
And the Carpathian wizard's hook,

852 *the old swain*: Meliboeus.   854 *warbled*: see Nativity Ode,
l. 96, etc.   857 *hard-besetting need*: danger or necessity threatening
closely.   858 *adjuring*: invoking or imploring.   862 *braids*: plaits,
wreaths. See l. 105.   *knitting*: intertwining.   763 *train*: flowing
length.   *amber-dropping*: shedding perfume; cf. l. 106.   869 *mace*:
trident.   872 *hook*: crook.

By scaly Triton's winding shell
And old sooth-saying Glaucus' spell,
By Leucothea's lovely hands
And her son that rules the strands,
By Thetis' tinsel-slipper'd feet
And the songs of Sirens sweet,
By dead Parthenope's dear tomb
And fair Ligea's golden comb,   880
Wherewith she sits on diamond rocks
Sleeking her soft alluring locks;
By all the nymphs that nightly dance
Upon thy streams with wily glance;
Rise, rise, and heave thy rosy head
From thy coral-paven bed,
And bridle in thy headlong wave
Till thou our summons answer'd have:
    Listen and save!

Sabrina *rises, attended by water-nymphs, and sings:*

By the rushy-fringèd bank   890
Where grows the willow and the osier dank,
  My sliding chariot stays,
Thick-set with agate and the azurn sheen
Of turkis blue and emerald green
  That in the channel strays,
Whilst from off the waters fleet
Thus I set my printless feet

873 *winding shell*: shell trumpet.   885 *heave*: lift up.   887 *bridle in*: rein in, check.   892 *stays*: halts.   893 *azurn*: azure (a clear blue).   894 *turkis*: turquoise.   895 *That ... strays*: i.e. the blue and green water that ripples down the river-bed.   896 *from off*: moving away from.   *fleet*: swift.   897 *printless*: leaving no print

O'er the cowslip's velvet head,
That bends not as I tread;
Gentle swain, at thy request   900
  I am here.

Spirit. Goddess dear,
We implore thy powerful hand
To undo the charmèd band
Of true virgin here distress'd
Through the force and through the wile
Of unblest enchanter vile.
Sabrina. Shepherd, 'tis my office best
To help ensnarèd chastity.
Brightest Lady, look on me: 910
Thus I sprinkle on thy breast
Drops that from my fountain pure
I have kept of precious cure,
Thrice upon thy finger's tip,
Thrice upon thy rubied lip;
Next this marble venom'd seat
Smear'd with gums of glutinous heat,
I touch with chaste palms moist and cold;
Now the spell hath lost his hold,
And I must haste ere morning hour   920
To wait in Amphitrite's bower.

Sabrina *descends, and the* Lady *rises out of her seat.*

Spirit. Virgin, daughter of Locrine,
Sprung of old Anchises' line,

903 *powerful*: wonder-working.   904 *band*: bondage.   908 *office
best*: best function.   910 *Brightest*: fairest.   913 *of precious cure*:
precious because they have power to cure.   916 *venom'd seat*: i.e.
the 'enchanted chair' in which the Lady is 'fix'd and motionless' (l. 819).
917 *glutinous*: adhesive.   921 *wait*: attend, pay homage.   *bower*:
see l. 45, and *L'Allegro*, l. 87, *Il Penseroso*, l. 27, etc.

May thy brimmèd waves for this
Their full tribute never miss
From a thousand petty rills
That tumble down the snowy hills:
Summer drouth or singèd air
Never scorch thy tresses fair,
Nor wet October's torrent flood   930
Thy molten crystal fill with mud;
May thy billows roll ashore
The beryl and the golden ore;
May thy lofty head be crown'd
With many a tower and terrace round,
And here and there, thy banks upon,
With groves of myrrh and cinnamon.

   Come Lady, while Heaven lends us grace,
Let us fly this cursèd place,
Lest the sorcerer us entice   940
With some other new device.
Not a waste or needless sound,
Till we come to holier ground:
I shall be your faithful guide
Through this gloomy covert wide,
And not many furlongs thence
Is your father's residence;
Where this night are met in state
Many a friend to gratulate
His wish'd presence, and beside   950
All the swains that there abide

924 *brimmèd*: brimming.   928 *singèd*: parched with heat.
929 *tresses fair*: i.e. the waves of the river.   933 *beryl*: a semi-
precious stone.   938 *lends us grace*: favours us.   941 *device*: cunning trick.   942 *waste*: superfluous. See l. 729.   945 *covert*: thick
wood.   949 *gratulate*: give thanks for.   950 *beside*:
besides.

With jigs and rural dance resort.
We shall catch them at their sport,
And our sudden coming there
Will double all their mirth and cheer.
Come let us haste, the stars grow high,
But night sits monarch yet in the mid sky.

The Scene changes, presenting Ludlow *Town and the President's Castle. Then come in country-dancers; after them the* Attendant Spirit *with the two* Brothers *and the* Lady.

SONG

Spirit. *Back, shepherds, back, enough your play*
Till next sunshine holiday.
Here be, without duck or nod,   960
Other trippings to be trod
Of lighter toes, and such court guise
As Mercury did first devise
With the mincing Dryades
On the lawns and on the leas.

This second Song presents them to their father and mother:

Noble Lord and Lady bright,
I have brought ye new delight:
Here behold so goodly grown
Three fair branches of your own.
Heaven hath timely tried their youth,   970
Their faith, their patience and their truth;

953 *sport*: merrymaking.   956 *the stars grow high*: i.e. it is late, the stars having risen towards the zenith.   959 *sunshine holiday*: see *L'Allegro*, l. 98.   960 *duck or nod*: rustic curtsey and bow.   961 *trippings*: dances.   962 *guise*: fashion.   964 *mincing*: neat-footed, taking dainty steps.   965 *leas*: meadows.   970 *timely*: early. *tried*: tested. Cf. l. 806.

And sent them here through hard assays
With a crown of deathless praise,
　To triumph in victorious dance
O'er sensual Folly and Intemperance.

　The dances ended, the Spirit *epiloguizes.*

Spirit. To the Ocean now I fly,
And those happy climes that lie
Where day never shuts his eye,
Up in the broad fields of the sky.
There I suck the liquid air   980
All amidst the gardens fair
Of Hesperus, and his daughters three
That sing about the golden tree:
Along the crispèd shades and bowers
Revels the spruce and jocund Spring,
The Graces and the rosy-bosom'd Hours
Thither all their bounties bring;
There eternal Summer dwells,
And west winds with musky wing
About the cedarn alleys fling   990
Nard and cassia's balmy smells.
Iris there with humid bow
Waters the odorous banks that blow
Flowers of more mingled hue
Than her purfled scarf can shew;
And drenches with Elysian dew
(List mortals, if your ears be true)

972 *assays*: trials.   977 *climes*: regions.   980 *suck*: breathe in.
984 *Along*: through. Cf. l. 844.   *crispèd*: curly, wreathed.   985 *spruce*:
lively.   989 *musky*: perfumed.   990 *cedarn*: cedar.   991 *Nard*
and cassia: sweet spices.   993 *blow*: bloom with.   995 *purfled*:
embroidered.   *scarf*: band of silk.   *shew*: show. Cf. l. 512.   997 *true*:
attuned (i.e. attentive) to truth.

Beds of hyacinth and roses
Where young Adonis oft reposes,
Waxing well of his deep wound   1000
In slumber soft, and on the ground
Sadly sits the Assyrian queen.
But far above in spangled sheen
Celestial Cupid, her famed son advanced,
Holds his dear Psyche sweet entranced
After her wandering labours long,
Till free consent the gods among
Make her his eternal bride,
And from her fair unspotted side
Two blissful twins are to be born,   1010
Youth and Joy; so Jove hath sworn.
  But now my task is smoothly done,
I can fly or I can run
Quickly to the green earth's end
Where the bow'd welkin slow doth bend,
And from thence can soar as soon
To the corners of the moon.
  Mortals that would follow me,
Love Virtue, she alone is free.
She can teach ye how to climb   1020
Higher than the sphery chime;
Or if Virtue feeble were,
Heaven itself would stoop to her.

1000 *Waxing well*: recovering.   1003 *spangled sheen*: starlight.
1004 *advanced*: promoted, exalted.   1009 *unspotted*: pure.   *side*:
womb.   1012 *smoothly*: successfully.   1015 *bow'd welkin*: arched
sky, firmament.   1018 *would*: wish to.   1021 *the sphery chime*:
the music of the spheres.   1022 *feeble*: unable to prevail.   1023 *stoop
to*: bend down (to help).

Lycidas

In this Monody the Author bewails a learned Friend,
unfortunately drowned in his passage from Chester on the
Irish Seas, 1637; and by occasion foretells the ruin
of our corrupted Clergy, then in their height.

YET once more, O ye laurels, and once more
Ye myrtles brown, with ivy never sere,
I come to pluck your berries harsh and crude,
And with forced fingers rude
Shatter your leaves before the mellowing year.
Bitter constraint and sad occasion dear
Compels me to disturb your season due:
For Lycidas is dead, dead ere his prime,
Young Lycidas, and hath not left his peer.
Who would not sing for Lycidas? he knew   10
Himself to sing, and build the lofty rhyme.
He must not float upon his watery bier
Unwept, and welter to the parching wind
Without the meed of some melodious tear.
  Begin then, Sisters of the sacred well
That from beneath the seat of Jove doth spring,
Begin, and somewhat loudly sweep the string;
Hence with denial vain and coy excuse!
So may some gentle Muse
With lucky words favour my destined urn,   20

2 *brown*: dusky. Cf. *Il Penseroso*, l. 134.   *sere*: withered.   3 *crude*:
unripe.   4 *forced*: compelled.   *rude*: rough, unskilled.   6 *constraint*:
compulsion.   *dear*: rousing deep emotion.   9 *peer*: equal.   11 *rhyme*:
poem.   13 *welter*: roll about.   14 *meed*: tribute.   *melodious tear*:
elegy.   19 *Muse*: poet (as inspired by a muse).

And as he passes turn
And bid fair peace be to my sable shroud.
For we were nursed upon the self-same hill,
Fed the same flock, by fountain, shade and rill.

   Together both, ere the high lawns appear'd
Under the opening eyelids of the morn,
We drove afield, and both together heard
What time the gray-fly winds her sultry horn,
Battening our flocks with the fresh dews of night
Oft till the star that rose at evening bright   30
Toward Heaven's descent had sloped his westering wheel.
Meanwhile the rural ditties were not mute,
Temper'd to the oaten flute;
Rough Satyrs danced, and Fauns with cloven heel
From the glad sound would not be absent long,
And old Damoetas loved to hear our song.

   But O the heavy change, now thou art gone,
Now thou art gone and never must return!
Thee Shepherd, thee the woods and desert caves,
With wild thyme and the gadding vine o'ergrown,   40
And all their echoes mourn.
The willows and the hazel copses green
Shall now no more be seen
Fanning their joyous leaves to thy soft lays.
As killing as the canker to the rose,
Or taint-worm to the weanling herds that graze,
Or frost to flowers that their gay wardrop wear

   25 *high lawns*: grassy slopes or hill-tops.   28 *What time*: at that
time when.   *winds*: blows, sounds.   29 *Battening*: feeding. Cf. *Hamlet*,
III. iv.   30 *the star that rose*: i.e. Hesperus.   31 *westering*: moving
to the west.   33 *Temper'd*: attuned.   *oaten flute*: shepherd's pipe.
39 *desert*: lonely.   40 *gadding*: wandering (as putting out tendrils).
44 *lays*: songs.   46 *weanling*: newly weaned.   47 *wardrop*: ward-
robe, clothes.

When first the white-thorn blows:
Such, Lycidas, thy loss to shepherd's ear.
 Where were ye Nymphs, when the remorseless deep 50
Closed o'er the head of your loved Lycidas?
For neither were ye playing on the steep
Where your old bards, the famous Druids lie,
Nor on the shaggy top of Mona high,
Nor yet where Deva spreads her wizard stream.
Ay me, I fondly dream!
Had ye been there—for what could that have done?
What could the Muse herself that Orpheus bore,
The Muse herself, for her enchanting son
Whom universal Nature did lament,   60
When by the rout that made the hideous roar
His gory visage down the stream was sent,
Down the swift Hebrus to the Lesbian shore?
 Alas! What boots it with uncessant care
To tend the homely slighted shepherd's trade,
And strictly meditate the thankless Muse?
Were it not better done as others use,
To sport with Amaryllis in the shade
Or with the tangles of Neaera's hair?
Fame is the spur that the clear spirit doth raise   70
(That last infirmity of noble mind)
To scorn delights and live laborious days;
But the fair guerdon when we hope to find
And think to burst out into sudden blaze,

48 *blows*: blooms.   52 *steep*: mountain.   54 *shaggy*: wooded.
55 *wizard*: winding.   56 *fondly*: foolishly.   61 *rout*: rabble,
disorderly crowd.   64 *What boots it*: what advantage does it bring?
uncessant: incessant.   65 *slighted*: despised.   66 *strictly*: unswerv-
ingly.   *meditate*: study. Cf. *Comus*, l. 547.   67 *use*: are accustomed
to do. Cf. l. 136.   70 *clear*: pure, noble.   *raise*: rouse, urge.
73 *guerdon*: reward.   74 *blaze*: fame, renown.

Comes the blind Fury with the abhorrèd shears,
And slits the thin-spun life. 'But not the praise,'
Phoebus replied, and touch'd my trembling ears:
'Fame is no plant that grows on mortal soil,
Nor in the glistering foil
Set off to the world, nor in broad rumour lies,   80
But lives and spreads aloft by those pure eyes
And perfect witness of all-judging Jove;
As he pronounces lastly on each deed,
Of so much fame in Heaven expect thy meed.'

  O fountain Arethuse, and thou honour'd flood,
Smooth-sliding Mincius, crown'd with vocal reeds,
That strain I heard was of a higher mood:
But now my oat proceeds,
And listens to the Herald of the Sea
That came in Neptune's plea.   90
He ask'd the waves, and ask'd the felon winds,
What hard mishap hath doom'd this gentle swain?
And question'd every gust of rugged wings
That blows from off each beakèd promontory;
They knew not of his story;
And sage Hippotades their answer brings,
That not a blast was from his dungeon stray'd,
The air was calm, and on the level brine
Sleek Panope with all her sisters play'd.
It was that fatal and perfidious bark,   100

---

79 *foil*: setting of metal to show off a gem.   80 *broad*: widespread.
81 *by*: 'by means of' or 'in sight of'.   82 *witness*: knowledge, awareness.   83 *pronounces lastly*: gives final judgement.   84 *meed*:
award. See l. 14.   88 'But now I return to the pastoral mood and theme.'
oat: shepherd's pipe. See l. 35 n. and *Comus*, l. 345.   90 *in Neptune's
plea*: to plead Neptune's defence (against the accusation of having caused
the death of Lycidas).   91 *felon*: wicked.   95 'They did not
know what he was talking about.'   98 *brine*: sea.

Built in the eclipse and rigg'd with curses dark,
That sunk so low that sacred head of thine.

  Next Camus, reverend sire, went footing slow,
His mantle hairy and his bonnet sedge,
Inwrought with figures dim, and on the edge
Like to that sanguine flower inscribed with woe.
'Ah! who hath reft' (quoth he) 'my dearest pledge?'
Last came, and last did go,
The Pilot of the Galilean Lake;
Two massy keys he bore of metals twain   110
(The golden opes, the iron shuts amain);
He shook his mitred locks, and stern bespake:
'How well could I have spared for thee, young swain,
Enow of such as for their bellies' sake
Creep and intrude and climb into the fold!
Of other care they little reckoning make
Than how to scramble at the shearer's feast
And shove away the worthy bidden guest.
Blind mouths! that scarce themselves know how to hold
A sheep-hook, or have learnt aught else the least   120
That to the faithful herdman's art belongs!
What recks it them? What need they? They are sped;
And when they list, their lean and flashy songs
Grate on their scrannel pipes of wretched straw:

---

103 *footing*: walking.   105 *figures dim*: mysterious images or pictures.   106 *sanguine*: blood-coloured.   107 *reft*: snatched away.   *pledge*: precious possession (used especially of a child; Latin, *pignus*). Cf. *At a Solemn Music*, l. 1.   110 *massy*: massive.   111 *amain*: strongly, emphatically.   113 *for thee*: instead of thee.   *swain*: country youth.   114 *Enow*: plural of 'enough'.   116 *care*: work, duty.
120 *aught else the least*: anything else, however easy.   122 *What recks it them?* What do they care? Cf. *Comus*, l. 404.   *They are sped*: they are provided for.   123 *when they list*: when it pleases them (to preach). *lean*: meagre, thin-toned; the songs, i.e. sermons, are lacking in substance. *flashy*: specious.   124 *scrannel*: thin, feeble.

The hungry sheep look up and are not fed,
But swoll'n with wind and the rank mist they draw,
Rot inwardly, and foul contagion spread;
Besides what the grim wolf with privy paw
Daily devours apace, and nothing said.
But that two-handed engine at the door   130
Stands ready to smite once, and smite no more.'

   Return, Alpheus, the dread voice is past
That shrunk thy streams; return, Sicilian Muse,
And call the vales, and bid them hither cast
Their bells and flowerets of a thousand hues.
Ye valleys low where the mild whispers use
Of shades and wanton winds and gushing brooks,
On whose fresh lap the swart star sparely looks;
Throw hither all your quaint enamell'd eyes
That on the green turf suck the honey'd showers,   140
And purple all the ground with vernal flowers.
Bring the rathe primrose that forsaken dies,
The tufted crow-toe and pale jessamine,
The white pink and the pansy freak'd with jet,
The glowing violet,
The musk-rose and the well-attired woodbine,
With cowslips wan that hang the pensive head,
And every flower that sad embroidery wears;
Bid Amaranthus all his beauty shed,

  126 *rank*: sour.   *draw*: breathe in.   **128** *privy*: secret.   **129** *and nothing said*: without any protest.   **130** *engine*: weapon.   **133** *shrunk*: made shrink, frightened.   **136** *use*: dwell, haunt.   **137** *shades*: woods. *wanton*: playful.   **138** *swart*: dark. *sparely looks*: hardly, or rarely, shines.   **139** *quaint*: curiously decorated. *enamell'd*: brightly coloured.   **141** *purple*: empurple, enrich with colour. *vernal*: springtime.   **142** *rathe*: early. *forsaken*: neglected. Cf. *Winter's Tale*, IV. iii.   **144** *freak'd*: freckled or spotted.   **146** *well-attired*: handsomely dressed or crowned. Cf. *On Time*, l. 20.   **148** *sad*: sober, not gaudy.

And daffadillies fill their cups with tears,   150
To strew the laureate hearse where Lycid lies:
For so to interpose a little ease
Let our frail thoughts dally with false surmise.
Ay me! whilst thee the shores and sounding seas
Wash far away, where'er thy bones are hurl'd,
Whether beyond the stormy Hebrides
Where thou perhaps under the whelming tide
Visit'st the bottom of the monstrous world;
Or whether thou, to our moist vows denied,
Sleep'st by the fable of Bellerus old   160
Where the great Vision of the guarded Mount
Looks toward Namancos and Bayona's hold:
Look homeward Angel now, and melt with ruth;
And O ye dolphins, waft the hapless youth.
    Weep no more, woeful shepherds, weep no more,
For Lycidas your sorrow is not dead,
Sunk though he be beneath the watery floor;
So sinks the day-star in the ocean bed,
And yet anon repairs his drooping head
And tricks his beams, and with new-spangled ore   170
Flames in the forehead of the morning sky.
So Lycidas sunk low, but mounted high,

    151 *laureate*: decorated with laurel (the poet's crown).   *hearse*: bier.
153 *frail*: weak (as unable to face the truth).   *dally with false surmise*:
'linger over a fancy which we know to be baseless' (because the body of
Lycidas is lost).   154 *shores*: shallow waters on coasts.   *sounding*:
resounding.   157 *whelming*: engulfing.   158 *monstrous world*:
world where monsters live. Cf. *Comus*, l. 533.   159 *moist vows*:
prayers and tears. Cf. *Arcades*, l. 6.   160 *by the fable of Bellerus old*:
'where the story of Bellerus is supposed to have happened.'   162 *hold*:
fort.   164 *waft*: carry over the waves.   166 *your sorrow*: the cause
of your sorrow.   168 *the day-star*: the sun.   169 *anon*: shortly.
repairs: renews.   170 *tricks*: dresses (i.e. brightens up). Cf. *Il Penseroso*, l. 123.   *new-spangled*: newly shining.   *ore*: gold.

Through the dear might of him that walk'd the waves,
Where other groves and other streams along,
With nectar pure his oozy locks he laves,
And hears the unexpressive nuptial song
In the blest kingdoms meek of joy and love.
There entertain him all the saints above
In solemn troops and sweet societies
That sing, and singing in their glory move,   180
And wipe the tears for ever from his eyes.
Now Lycidas, the shepherds weep no more;
Henceforth thou art the Genius of the shore
In thy large recompense, and shalt be good
To all that wander in that perilous flood.

  Thus sang the uncouth swain to the oaks and rills,
While the still Morn went out with sandals gray;
He touch'd the tender stops of various quills,
With eager thought warbling his Doric lay;
And now the sun had stretch'd out all the hills,   190
And now was dropp'd into the western bay.
At last he rose, and twitch'd his mantle blue:
Tomorrow to fresh woods and pastures new.

---

173 *dear might*: loving power.   174 *other*: i.e. other than those on earth.   175 *oozy*: wet (from the sea).   *laves*: washes. Cf. 'lavers', *Comus*, l. 838.   176 *unexpressive*: inexpressible.   183 *Genius*: local god.   184 *thy large recompense*: the generous recompense made to you (by God).   *good*: kind, helpful.   186 *uncouth*: unskilful. 188 *tender*: loving.   *stops*: holes of a flute or pipe.   *various quills*: differing pipes of a shepherd's flute.   190 *stretch'd out all the hills*: lengthened the shadows of the hills.   192 *twitch'd*: pulled together, adjusted.

SONNETS

I

To the Nightingale

O NIGHTINGALE, that on yon bloomy spray
   Warblest at eve, when all the woods are still,
   Thou with fresh hope the lover's heart dost fill
   While the jolly hours lead on propitious May;
Thy liquid notes that close the eye of day,   5
   First heard before the shallow cuckoo's bill,
   Portend success in love. O if Jove's will
   Have link'd that amorous power to thy soft lay,
Now timely sing, ere the rude bird of hate
   Foretell my hopeless doom in some grove nigh;   10
   As thou from year to year hast sung too late
For my relief, yet hadst no reason why:
   Whether the Muse or Love call thee his mate,
   Both them I serve, and of their train am I.

II

On His being Arrived to the Age of
Twenty-Four

HOW soon hath Time, the subtle thief of youth,
   Stol'n on his wing my three-and-twentieth year!

I. 4 *jolly*: smiling, comely. See *Comus*, l. 986.   *propitious*: i.e. to the
lover.   6 *shallow*: thin-sounding. *bill*: for 'voice'.   8 *amorous
power*: power over love.   9 *timely*: early, in time. *bird of hate*:
i.e. the cuckoo.   13 *mate*: companion; 'his' refers to the god of
love, the Muse being feminine.   14 *train*: crowd of followers.

My hasting days fly on with full career,
But my late spring no bud or blossom shew'th.
Perhaps my semblance might deceive the truth   5
   That I to manhood am arrived so near,
   And inward ripeness doth much less appear,
   That some more timely-happy spirits endu'th.
Yet be it less or more, or soon or slow,
   It shall be still in strictest measure even   10
   To that same lot, however mean or high,
Toward which Time leads me, and the will of Heaven;
   All is, if I have grace to use it so,
   As ever in my great Task-Master's eye.

III

When the Assault was Intended to the City

CAPTAIN or Colonel, or Knight in arms,
   Whose chance on these defenceless doors may seize,
   If deed of honour did thee ever please,
   Guard them, and him within protect from harms.

II. 3 *career*: speed.   4 *shew'th*: for this spelling and pronunciation see *Comus*, ll. 512, 995.   5 *semblance*: appearance. *deceive the truth*: mislead as to the truth.   8 *more timely-happy*: flourishing earlier. *endu'th*: leads on.   9 *it*: i.e. inward ripeness.   10 *still*: continually. *even*: adjusted, responsive.   11 *that same lot*: that precise way of life.   13–14 'All my life is always as it were under the eyes of God, if I have the grace to use it in that way.'

III. 1 *Colonel*: Milton prefers a pronunciation based on the Italian origin of the word (derived from *colonna*, a column).   2 *Whose chance*: who by chance (i.e. fortune).

He can requite thee; for he knows the charms 5
   That call fame on such gentle acts as these,
   And he can spread thy name o'er lands and seas,
   Whatever clime the sun's bright circle warms.
Lift not thy spear against the Muses' bower:
   The great Emathian conqueror bid spare 10
   The house of Pindarus, when temple and tower
Went to the ground; and the repeated air
   Of sad Electra's poet had the power
   To save the Athenian walls from ruin bare.

IV

To a Virtuous Young Lady

LADY that in the prime of earliest youth
   Wisely hast shunn'd the broad way and the green,
   And with those few art eminently seen
   That labour up the hill of heavenly Truth:
The better part with Mary and with Ruth 5
   Chosen thou hast; and they that overween,
   And at thy growing virtues fret their spleen,
   No anger find in thee, but pity and ruth.

5 *charms*: meaning both 'songs' and 'spells' (Latin, *carmina*).   6 *gentle*: kind, civilized. See *Comus*, l. 236.   8 *clime*: region. Cf. *Arcades*, l. 24, and *Comus*, l. 977.   *circle*: course.   9 *bower*: dwelling-place. See *Comus*, l. 45.   12 *the repeated air*: the repetition of the air. For the Latin construction see also *Comus*, l. 48.

IV. 3 *eminently seen*: seen as standing out.   6 *overween*: are presumptuous, or wise in their own conceit.   7 *fret their spleen*: vex themselves with malice.

Thy care is fix'd, and zealously attends
  To fill thy odorous lamp with deeds of light,   10
  And hope that reaps not shame. Therefore be sure
Thou, when the Bridegroom with his feastful friends
  Passes to bliss at the mid-hour of night,
  Hast gain'd thy entrance, Virgin wise and pure.

V

To the Lady Margaret Ley

DAUGHTER to that good Earl, once President
  Of England's Council and her Treasury,
  Who lived in both unstain'd with gold or fee,
  And left them both, more in himself content,
Till the sad breaking of that Parliament   5
  Broke him, as that dishonest victory
  At Chaeronea, fatal to liberty,
  Kill'd with report that old man eloquent:
Though later born than to have known the days
  Wherein your father flourish'd, yet by you,   10
  Madam, methinks I see him living yet;
So well your words his noble virtues praise
  That all both judge you to relate them true,
  And to possess them, honour'd Margaret.

9 *Thy care is fix'd*: your purpose is unchanging.   *attends*: pays attention.   11 *reaps not shame*: does not incur shame as a consequence.
12 *feastful*: rejoicing.   13 *bliss*: blessedness, the perfect joy of Heaven.
14 *thy entrance*: i.e. into bliss with the Bridegroom.

V. 3 *unstain'd with gold or fee*: untainted by bribery.   *fee*: property of value.   4 *more in himself content*: preferring retirement and his own thoughts (even to honourable public life).   5 *breaking*: forcible termination.   6 *dishonest*: shameful.   8 *with report*: by its being reported.   10 *by you*: by means of you.

VI

On the Detraction which followed upon my Writing certain Treatises

A BOOK was writ of late call'd *Tetrachordon*,
    And woven close, both matter, form and style;
    The subject new, it walk'd the town a while,
    Numbering good intellects; now seldom pored on.
Cries the stall-reader, 'Bless us! what a word on   5
    A title-page is this!' and some in file
    Stand spelling false, while one might walk to Mile-
    End Green. Why is it harder, Sirs, than *Gordon*,
Colkitto, or *Macdonnel*, or *Galasp*?
    Those rugged names to our like mouths grow sleek   10
    That would have made Quintilian stare and gasp.
Thy age, like ours, O soul of Sir John Cheek,
    Hated not learning worse than toad or asp,
    When thou taught'st Cambridge and King Edward Greek.

VII

On the Same

I DID but prompt the age to quit their clogs
    By the known rules of ancient liberty,

VI. 2 *woven close*: carefully worked out.   3 *The subject new*: while
the subject was new.   4 *Numbering*: counting up (among its readers).
5 *stall-reader*: reader at booksellers' stalls.   6 *in file*: in a row.   7 *spelling false*: Cf. *Il Penseroso*, l. 170.   10 *rugged*: rough, harsh.   *like
mouths*: equally rough (i.e. barbarous) mouths.   *sleek*: smooth, i.e. easy.
13 *Hated not . . . asp*: i.e. they did not hate learning more than toad or
asp, but 'as much as they hated either'.   *asp*: a venomous snake.
    VII. 1 *prompt*: urge.   *the age*: the present time.   *quit their clogs*: get
rid of their hindrances.   2 *By*: according to.

When straight a barbarous noise environs me
　　Of owls and cuckoos, asses, apes and dogs;
As when those hinds that were transform'd to frogs   5
　　Rail'd at Latona's twin-born progeny,
　　Which after held the sun and moon in fee.
　　But this is got by casting pearl to hogs,
That bawl for freedom in their senseless mood
　　And still revolt when truth would set them free.   10
　　Licence they mean when they cry Liberty;
For who loves that, must first be wise and good;
　　But from that mark how far they rove we see,
　　For all this waste of wealth and loss of blood.

VIII

To Mr. Henry Lawes, on His Airs

HARRY, whose tuneful and well-measured song
　　First taught our English music how to span
　　Words with just note and accent, not to scan
　　With Midas' ears, committing short and long;
Thy worth and skill exempts thee from the throng,   5
　　With praise enough for Envy to look wan;
　　To after-age thou shalt be writ the man
　　That with smooth air couldst humour best our tongue.

3 *environs*: surrounds.　　5 *hinds*: rustics.　　6 *Rail'd at*: insulted.
7 *after*: afterwards. Cf. Sonnet XVII, l. 6.　　*in fee*: as a fief or domain.
13 *that mark*: that target (of virtue).　*rove*: aim aside. To 'rove' an arrow
at a target was to aim allowing for the wind.　　14 *For*: i.e. from.

VIII. 1 *well-measured*: skilfully rhythmic. See *Arcades*, l. 71.　2 *span*:
yoke, link together.　　3 *scan*: count syllables in verse.　　4 *committing*: setting at variance.　*short and long*: i.e. short syllables and long
notes, or vice versa.　　5 *exempts*: singles out, distinguishes.　7 *after-age*: posterity.　*writ the man*: recorded as the man.　　8 *air*: song.
humour: fit, suit the nature of.

Thou honour'st verse, and verse must lend her wing
  To honour thee, the priest of Phoebus' quire,   10
  That tun'st their happiest lines in hymn or story.
Dante shall give Fame leave to set thee higher
  Than his Casella, whom he woo'd to sing,
  Met in the milder shades of Purgatory.

IX

On the Religious Memory of Mrs Catharine Thomason, my Christian Friend, Deceased December, 1646.

WHEN Faith and Love, which parted from thee never,
  Had ripen'd thy just soul to dwell with God,
  Meekly thou didst resign this earthy load
Of Death, call'd Life, which us from Life doth sever.
Thy works and alms and all thy good endeavour   5
  Stay'd not behind, nor in the grave were trod;
  But as Faith pointed with her golden rod
Follow'd thee up to joy and bliss for ever.
Love led them on, and Faith who knew them best
  Thy handmaids, clad them o'er with purple beams   10
  And azure wings, that up they flew so dress'd,
And spake the truth of thee in glorious themes
  Before the Judge, who thenceforth bid thee rest,
  And drink thy fill of pure immortal streams.

---

9 *lend her wing*: help with her inspiration.   10 *priest of Phoebus' quire*: ministering to poets.   11 *their*: i.e. the poets'.   *happiest*: most inspired.   13 *woo'd*: begged.

IX. 10 *Thy handmaids*: i.e. to be thy handmaids.   11 *dress'd*: adorned. 12 *themes*: strains of music.

X

On the New Forcers of Conscience under the Long Parliament

BECAUSE you have thrown off your Prelate Lord,
 And with stiff vows renounced his Liturgy,
 To seize the widow'd whore Plurality
From them whose sin ye envied, not abhorr'd;
Dare ye for this adjure the civil sword   5
 To force our consciences that Christ set free,
 And ride us with a classic hierarchy
Taught ye by mere A. S. and Rotherford?
Men whose life, learning, faith and pure intent
 Would have been held in high esteem with Paul 10
 Must now be named and printed heretics
By shallow Edwards and Scotch What-d'ye-call.
 But we do hope to find out all your tricks,
 Your plots and packings, worse than those of Trent,
   That so the Parliament   15
 May with their wholesome and preventive shears
 Clip your phylacteries, though baulk your ears,
   And succour our just fears,
 When they shall read this clearly in your charge:
 New Presbyter is but old Priest writ large.   20

X. 2 *stiff*: solemn. 3 *Plurality*: the practice of holding more than
one church benefice. 5 *adjure*: exhort, admonish. *the civil sword*: the
lay authorities, i.e. Parliament. See Sonnet XIII, l. 12. 7 *ride*: saddle.
hierarchy: ruling body of clerics organized into grades. 8 *mere*
A. S.: 'somebody calling himself only A.S.' (with a pun on 'mere ass').
11 *printed*: denounced in print. 12 *shallow*: half educated. *What-d'ye-
call*: What's-his-name. 14 *packings*: packed votes. 17 *baulk*: spare,
stop short at. 18 *succour*: bring relief to. 19 *in your charge*: as an
accusation against you. 20 *large*: in full. 'Priest' is a contracted form of
'presbyter', both being derived from the Greek *presbyteros*.

XI

On the Lord General Fairfax, at the Siege of Colchester

FAIRFAX, whose name in arms through Europe rings
   Filling each mouth with envy or with praise,
   And all her jealous monarchs with amaze
   And rumours loud, that daunt remotest kings;
Thy firm unshaken virtue ever brings   5
   Victory home, though new rebellions raise
   Their Hydra heads, and the false North displays
   Her broken league, to imp their serpent wings.
O yet a nobler task awaits thy hand:
   For what can war but endless war still breed,   10
   Till truth and right from violence be freed,
And public faith clear'd from the shameful brand
   Of public fraud? In vain doth Valour bleed,
   While Avarice and Rapine share the land.

XI. 1 *name in arms*: fame in war.   3 *jealous*: suspicious.   5 *unshaken*: unshakable.   *virtue*: valour (Lat. *virtus*).   7 *displays*: flaunts.
8 *league*: sworn faith.   *imp*: strengthen. To imp a hawk's wing was to
add a new piece of feather, to strengthen or repair it.   12 *brand*:
accusation.   14 *Rapine*: plunder.

XII

To the Lord General Cromwell, on the Proposals of certain Ministers at the Committee for Propagation of the Gospel. May, 1652

CROMWELL, our chief of men, who through a cloud
    Not of war only, but detractions rude,
    Guided by faith and matchless fortitude,
    To peace and truth thy glorious way hast plough'd,
And on the neck of crownèd Fortune proud   5
    Hast rear'd God's trophies and his work pursued,
    While Darwen stream with blood of Scots imbrued
    And Dunbar field resounds thy praises loud,
And Worcester's laureate wreath: yet much remains
    To conquer still; Peace hath her victories   10
    No less renown'd than war; new foes arise,
Threatening to bind our souls with secular chains.
    Help us to save free conscience from the paw
    Of hireling wolves whose Gospel is their maw.

XIII

To Sir Henry Vane the Younger

VANE, young in years but in sage counsel old,
    Than whom a better senator ne'er held

XII. 2 *detractions*: slanders.   6 *rear'd*: raised. Cf. *Comus*, l. 836.
trophies: arms and other spoils of war heaped as a monument of victory.
7 *imbrued*: stained.   8 *field*: battlefield.   12 *secular chains*: restrictions
imposed by the civil power. See Sonnet X, l. 5.   14 *hireling*: mercenary.
maw: belly, greed.
    XIII. 1 *sage counsel*: wise advice.

The helm of Rome, when gowns not arms repell'd
The fierce Epirot and the African bold;
Whether to settle peace or to unfold   5
The drift of hollow states, hard to be spell'd,
Then to advise how war may best, upheld,
Move by her two main nerves, iron and gold,
In all her equipage; besides to know
Both spiritual power and civil, what each means,   10
What severs each, thou hast learnt, which few have done.
The bounds of either sword to thee we owe;
Therefore on thy firm hand Religion leans
In peace, and reckons thee her eldest son.

XIV

On the late Massacre in Piemont

AVENGE O Lord thy slaughter'd saints, whose bones
Lie scatter'd on the Alpine mountains cold,
Even them who kept thy truth so pure of old
When all our fathers worshipp'd stocks and stones,
Forget not: in thy book record their groans,   5
Who were thy sheep, and in their ancient fold
Slain by the bloody Piemontese that roll'd
Mother with infant down the rocks. Their moans

3 *helm*: rudder, i.e. government.   *gowns*: togas (the dress of Roman
Senators).   5 *settle*: negotiate.   *unfold*: discover.   6 *drift*: hidden
meaning or aim.   *hollow*: false, hypocritical.   *spell'd*: interpreted.
7 *upheld*: if upheld, i.e. once decided on.   8 *nerves*: sinews.   *iron
and gold*: arms and money.   9 *equipage*: equipment, armament.
10 *civil*: secular.   11 *severs*: separates.   12 *bounds*: limits.   *either
sword*: i.e. either civil or spiritual authority.
    XIV. 4 *stocks and stones*: wooden and stone images.   6 *fold*: sheepfold.
7 *Piemontese*: Milton uses the Italian spelling and pronunciation for the
modern *Piedmont*.

The vales redoubled to the hills, and they
   To Heaven. Their martyr'd blood and ashes sow 10
   O'er all the Italian fields where still doth sway
The triple Tyrant; that from these may grow
   A hundredfold, who having learnt thy way
   Early may fly the Babylonian woe.

XV

On His Blindness

WHEN I consider how my light is spent,
   Ere half my days, in this dark world and wide,
   And that one talent which is death to hide
   Lodged with me useless, though my soul more bent
To serve therewith my Maker, and present   5
   My true account, lest he returning chide;
   'Doth God exact day-labour, light denied?'
   I fondly ask. But Patience, to prevent
That murmur, soon replies, 'God doth not need
   Either man's work or his own gifts. Who best   10
   Bear his mild yoke, they serve him best. His state
Is kingly: thousands at his bidding speed,
   And post o'er land and ocean without rest;
   They also serve who only stand and wait.'

9 *redoubled*: echoed.   11 *fields*: plains. Cf. *Comus*, l. 60.   *sway*:
hold sway, reign.

XV. 1 *spent*: extinguished (Italian, *spento*).   2 *Ere half my days*:
before half my life is over.   4 *Lodged with me*: given into my keeping.
bent: anxious.   8 *fondly*: foolishly.   *prevent*: forestall.   9 *murmur*:
complaint, expression of grievance.   11 *state*: Cf. *Comus*, l. 35.
12 *thousands*: i.e. of angels, spirits in God's service.   13 *post*: travel.
14 *stand and wait*: stand by (in readiness) and attend (as loyal subjects).

XVI

To Edward Lawrence

LAWRENCE, of virtuous father virtuous son,
　　Now that the fields are dank and ways are mire,
　　Where shall we sometimes meet, and by the fire
　　Help waste a sullen day, what may be won
From the hard season gaining? Time will run　　　5
　　On smoother, till Favonius reinspire
　　The frozen earth and clothe in fresh attire
　　The lily and rose, that neither sow'd nor spun.
What neat repast shall feast us, light and choice,
　　Of Attic taste, with wine, whence we may rise　10
　　To hear the lute well-touch'd, or artful voice
Warble immortal notes and Tuscan air?
　　He who of those delights can judge, and spare
　　To interpose them oft, is not unwise.

XVII

To Cyriack Skinner

CYRIACK, whose grandsire on the royal bench
　　Of British Themis with no mean applause
　　Pronounced, and in his volumes taught, our laws,
　　Which others at their bar so often wrench;

XVI. 1 *virtuous*: not only 'good', but 'able, talented' (as in the Latin use of *virtus*).　　4 *waste*: wear away, pass.　　5 *hard season*: winter. 6 *Favonius*: the west wind.　　9 *neat*: carefully prepared, elegant. 10 *whence we may rise*: after which we may rise from the table.　　11 *well-touch'd*: played well.　*artful*: well-trained.　　12 *Tuscan air*: Italian song. See *Comus*, l. 48.　　13 *spare*: forbear.　　14 *interpose them oft*: turn to them at frequent intervals (from more serious pursuits).

XVII. 2 *no mean*: much.　　3 *Pronounced*: interpreted.　　4 *at their bar*: in court.　*wrench*: twist, strain.

Today deep thoughts resolve with me to drench   5
  In mirth that after no repenting draws;
  Let Euclid rest, and Archimedes pause,
  And what the Swede intends, and what the French.
To measure life learn thou betimes, and know
  Toward solid good what leads the nearest way: 10
  For other things mild Heaven a time ordains,
And disapproves that care, though wise in show,
  That with superfluous burden loads the day,
  And when God sends a cheerful hour, refrains.

XVIII

To the Same

CYRIACK, this three years' day these eyes, though clear
  To outward view, of blemish or of spot,
  Bereft of light their seeing have forgot,
  Nor to their idle orbs doth sight appear
Of sun or moon or star throughout the year,   5
  Or man or woman. Yet I argue not
  Against Heaven's hand or will, nor bate a jot
  Of heart or hope, but still bear up and steer

---

5 *deep*: serious, problematic. *drench*: dissolve.   6 *mirth . . . draws*:
such pleasure as leads to no regrets.   9 *measure*: estimate. *betimes*:
early.   10 *solid*: real.   11 *For other things*: i.e. than 'deep thoughts'.
mild: kindly.   12 *care*: thoughtfulness. *though wise in show*: though
it may seem wise.   14 *refrains*: draws back (from the opportunity of
relaxation).

XVIII. 1 *this three years' day*: for the last three years.   4 *idle*: unused.
7 *Heaven's hand or will*: what God wills or has done. *bate*: abate, lessen.
a jot: the least part.   8–9 *bear up and steer Right onward*: sail forward
like a ship against the wind. To 'bear up' was to put the helm 'up' so as to
bring the vessel into the direction of the wind.

Right onward. What supports me, dost thou ask?
  The conscience, friend, to have lost them overplied   10
  In Liberty's defence, my noble task,
Of which all Europe talks from side to side.
  This thought might lead me through the world's vain mask
  Content though blind, had I no better guide.

XIX

On His Deceased Wife

METHOUGHT I saw my late espousèd saint
  Brought to me like Alcestis from the grave,
  Whom Jove's great son to her glad husband gave,
  Rescued from death by force, though pale and faint.
Mine as whom wash'd from spot of child-bed taint   5
  Purification in the Old Law did save,
  And such as yet once more I trust to have
  Full sight of her in Heaven without restraint,
Came vested all in white, pure as her mind:
  Her face was veil'd, yet to my fancied sight   10
  Love, sweetness, goodness, in her person shined
So clear, as in no face with more delight.
  But O as to embrace me she inclined
  I waked, she fled, and day brought back my night.

9 *supports me*: keeps up my courage.   10 *conscience*: consciousness. *overplied*: overworked.   13 *mask*: i.e. masque.

  XIX. 1 *saint*: 'Used in the double sense of "a good woman" and "a soul in heaven"' (Wright).   5 *Mine*: my wife.   5–6 *as whom . . . save*: 'like one whom purification . . . saved, having washed her. . . .'   8 *restraint*: hindrance.   9 *vested*: clothed.   10 *fancied sight*: sight I imagined I had.   12 *as . . . delight*: 'that one could have felt no greater delight in seeing any face'.   13 *inclined*: bent forward.   14 *fled*: vanished.

COMMENTARY

On the Morning of Christ's Nativity
(December 1629)

Until Milton wrote this poem at the age of 21 he had produced more Latin verse than English; his gifts as a scholar were obvious, but the Nativity Ode was his first great artistic success in his own language. It is packed with learning and full of literary reminiscences, but the manner is unmistakably Miltonic; that is, it foreshadows much in his later verse, in its rhythms, its feeling, its logical structure.

Spenser's influence appears in the introductory stanzas ending in Alexandrines, and in the use of Alexandrines to close the stanzas of the Hymn. But the latter are also shaped by Italian example: the combination and the grouping of three-stressed and five-stressed lines, in the first six lines of the stanzas, derive from the *canzone* tradition, and may have been suggested by the openings of many of Tasso's lyrics (e.g. *Parafrasi dell' inno Stabat Mater*); but the English stanza is shorter and swings along more quickly than is usual in Italian.

The content of the Hymn is also reminiscent of a Nativity poem by Tasso (*Pel presepio di nostro Signore nella cappella di Sisto V in s. Maria Maggiore*), which makes use of the supposed universal peace at the time of Christ's birth, and the overthrow of the pagan gods.

The subject had inspired centuries of religious poetry and art. Milton's treatment of it does not dwell on the intimate human or devotional feelings that could be stirred by the birth at Bethlehem, but concentrates on the Incarnation as a divinely ordained event that changes the course of history. The infant Jesus is a liberator, a spiritual champion who defeats sin and opens the way to salvation for Man; vast new perspectives stretch out from him into time and space.

There is fervent feeling, and a tenderness towards the shepherds and the child in the stable; but the young poet's religion is not only Biblical, but intellectual and philosophical. He is carried away by the idea of purity, aspiration, triumph over evil, which are imaged for him by music and light (as for Pythagoras and Plato). He hymns the victory of light over darkness, love and hope over cruelty and fear, in the battle for the soul of man.

The design and execution fit the theme of spiritual mastery; the poem is planned and controlled from beginning to end, with a vigour which sometimes forces transitions (see 149–56 n.) or results in an awkward 'conceit' (229–31). The introductory stanzas give the setting: the night of Christ's birth, the starlit sky before dawn, the Magi on the road to Bethlehem. After the vision of salvation, judgement, and the rout of sin, we return to the stable: the sun is now about to rise, all stands in readiness for the world's homage. The poem has the air of a daring exercise, a venture perfectly achieved, and we can sense the boyish delight of the poet in its success.

5. *holy sages*: the prophets of the Old Testament who foretold the coming of the Messiah.

23. *The star-led Wizards*: the Magi who were led by a star to the birth-place of Christ (St. Matthew 2). They offered the child in Bethlehem frankincense and myrrh ('odours sweet').

27. *angel quire*: the Shepherds in the fields of Bethlehem were told of the birth by a 'multitude of the heavenly host' (St. Luke 2). Some 60 lines of the Hymn (ll. 85–148) are inspired by the beauty of the angels' song.

28. In Isaiah 6 a seraph touches the prophet's lips with a live coal from the altar of God. In *The Reason of Church Government* (1642) Milton says that the poet must pray 'to that eternal Spirit who can enrich with all utterance and knowledge, and sends out his Seraphim with the hallowed fire of his Altar to touch and purify the lips of whom he pleases'.

29–31. *was . . . lies*: Throughout the poem, as in the preliminary stanzas, Milton combines the past with the present tense (see ll. 38, 46, 52; 61, 67; 70, 75, etc). While the latter can be described as 'the historic present', the effect is to make the Nativity an event both 'in and out of time'—an act of God continually renewed.

32–44. Nature puts on her winter dress partly in sympathy with Christ (who puts off his Godhead and assumes the nature of man), and partly to hide her imperfections from him. This idea is a 'conceit' like those found in the Metaphysical poets; but it has a solid core of meaning related to both theology and history: according to

Christian belief Nature shared in the corruption of man brought
about by the Fall. And when Christianity triumphed over the
pagan religion of the Roman Empire, it was a victory of this belief
over the worship of Nature in various forms. Thus the celebration
of Christmas replaced the pagan festival held just after midwinter
to celebrate the birth of a new Sun (after the winter solstice).

45–60. God sends peace on earth in preparation for the birth of
'the Prince of Peace' (see ll. 61–3). At the beginning of the Christian
era there was a general peace throughout the ancient world, for the
first time for many years; later this was interpreted by the Church
Fathers as a sign from Heaven.

68. *birds of calm*: halcyons, or kingfishers. 'Halcyon days', or days
of unexpected fine weather, were supposed to occur during a period
of seven days before and seven days after the winter solstice. The
sea was then calm, and allowed the halcyons to build their nest on
the waters and hatch their young.

71. *their precious influence*: According to astrological theory, the
stars and planets controlled, or at least had some effect on, the earth
and human affairs. Each exercised its power through an 'influence',
which was an 'inflowing' (in the literal Latin sense) of some invisible
and ethereal liquid or force. Such influences could of course be evil
as well as good, but Milton speaks only of the kind which was bene-
ficial, producing (for example) precious stones or metals in the
earth. The stars focus such good influences unanimously ('one way')
on Bethlehem. See *L'Allegro*, l. 122.

74. *Lucifer*: the morning-star ('light-bearing').

77–84. Like the conceit on winter (ll. 32–44), this fancy is based
both on the time of year and religious ideas. The sun rises late in
midwinter, but he is made to delay further because he feels that his
light and power are surpassed by God made Man, Christ, who brings
light and healing to the world. The sun was worshipped in many
pagan religions; as the greatest luminary, and one obviously bene-
ficial, if not the source of life itself, he was regarded as a God, or at
least as a symbol of divinity. In Christian tradition he stands for
Christ, not only because of his goodness to Nature, but because he
sets (i.e. dies) and rises again. At the moment of Christ's birth
however, he feels 'inferior' at the appearance of 'a greater sun'.

89. *Pan*: In classical pastorals Pan is the most important god, since

his domain was woods and pastures. When pastoral poetry becomes allegorical, the shepherds could be priests as well as poets, and Pan could represent Christ, the Good Shepherd. Spenser speaks of 'great Pan' or 'mighty Pan', meaning Christ, throughout *The Shepheardes Calender*; the reference to Pan in the May Eclogue (l. 54) has a footnote which may have contributed to ll. 173–80 of the Hymn (see n.).

90–1. The shepherds in pastoral verse are natural poets, whose usual theme is love.

101–3. The song of the angels to the shepherds is identified by Milton with the music of the spheres; this would not normally be heard below the sphere of the moon, as that was the level at which mortality, change and decay (characteristic of earth) began. 'The hollow round Of Cynthia's seat' is the sphere occupied by the moon. —The notion of the stars making music as they moved in their spheres comes from Plato (who derived it from Pythagoras); Plato said that it could be heard only by the soul of a man who was progressing through virtue to the contemplation of ultimate truth: he would be attuned to the harmony of the universe, and would be led on by it to the Eternal Beauty of God. See Appendix I.

107–8. See *Arcades*, ll. 63–73.

119. Compare Job 38: 7: 'When the morning stars sang together, and all the sons of God shouted for joy . . .'.

127. Compare *The Merchant of Venice*, v. i:

> There's not the smallest orb which thou behold'st
> But in his motion like an angel sings . . .
> Such harmony is in immortal souls,
> But whilst this muddy vesture of decay
> Doth grossly close it in, we cannot hear it.

131. *ninefold harmony*: There were eight spheres, each sounding a note of the musical octave; the ninth note or melody making up the harmony was a concentration of all the rest. (See Appendix I.) The Golden Age was placed in the remote past, before the Gods of Olympus dethroned Saturn, and Jove took his place. Man then enjoyed perpetual youth, war was unknown, the earth provided food, and work was unnecessary.

136. *speckled Vanity*: synonymous with the 'leprous Sin' of l. 138. 'Vanity' in Biblical usage means human mortality and sin.

138. *mould*: Compare *Comus*, l. 17.

139–40. Here Milton places Hell in the centre of the earth; in *Paradise Lost* it is in 'outer darkness'.

140. 'Peering' was used by the Elizabethans to mean 'overlooking'.

142. *down return*: Truth and Justice will come down to earth from Heaven, and dwell among men as they did in the Golden Age. The Greeks said that when the Golden Age ended, Astraea, the goddess of justice, had fled from the earth, but that one day she would return and re-establish her reign. Milton adds Mercy, thus making his version clearly Christian; it is a vision of the 'new Heavens, new earth' which Christ will bring at his Second Coming. But the next stanzas show it as premature, only a glimpse.

149–56. There are some turns of thought here which are logical in themselves, but perhaps too close to one another to be poetically effective. Providence decrees that the final redemption of Man and Nature must wait for Christ to complete his task of reconciling God and Man; it is now begun by his Incarnation, but can be achieved only by his Passion and Resurrection. His Resurrection guarantees the ultimate triumph over sin and death; but this will be ushered in only by the Last Judgement.

157–64. The prediction of the Day of Judgement is carried through a further stanza, but it brings us back to the point made in ll. 150–1, that the final Redemption of mankind 'now begins' (ll. 167). Stanzas XVI–XVIII are so closely linked as to form a unit, which is itself a link leading to the culminating passage of the Hymn, Stanzas XIX–XXVI.

158–9. See Exodus 19: 18: when Moses received the Ten Commandments, 'Mount Sinai was altogether on a smoke . . . and the whole mount quaked greatly'.

162. *centre*: See ll. 139–40 n.

164. *middle air*: Medieval science divided the air into three 'regions'. The middle air, above the lowest layer, reached to the tops of the highest mountains, and was the region of clouds, winds and storms; it was inhabited and largely controlled by demons, i.e. fallen angels. The upper air extended from the mountain tops to the moon; it was serene, and frequented by good spirit.

E

168–72. The Devil is given the form of a dragon in Revelation 12 and 20.

173–235. The curtailment of Satan's kingdom on earth is illustrated by the fear and flight of the pagan gods, at the birth of Christ. Milton dramatizes their defeat by making it instantaneous; the conversion of the Roman Empire in fact took several centuries. But the poem gains immeasurably from Milton's foreshortening of the time-scale: he combines historical events with the timeless, an eternal present; and this is not out of place even in the description of remote superstitions and barbaric cults. The coming of Christianity may have decided in advance the ultimate victory of good over evil. But human life was still to be a spiritual battlefield; the demons who had deceived men into worshipping them as Gods would continue to be active in less obvious ways.

173–80. The disarray of the pagan religions was founded on the Christian tradition concerning the failure of the Greek oracles; and Milton had read Spenser's *Shepheardes Calender*, where the notes on the May Eclogue relate a story, 'first recorded of Plutarch, in his booke of the ceasing of oracles'.—The oracle of Apollo at Delphi was the centre of Greek religion. When consulted through his priests, the God would give an answer (usually cryptic) through a prophetess who spoke in a trance or ecstasy. He might also communicate by means of a vision or a dream.

180. *pale-eyed*: The epithet evokes the expression of an ascetic, one who has purged his body by fasting or other means, in order to give greater freedom to his soul.

the prophetic cell: The innermost chamber of a temple, to which only priests and initiates had access; mysteries (i.e. secret rituals) took place there, and from it the god spoke in oracles.

181–8. The nature-spirits of Greek and Roman religion gave a supernatural aspect to landscape and country life. Woods, streams, mountains, and every particular locality had a presiding spirit, or *genius*; they were to linger on as local saints, or fairy superstitions, after the Christianization of the ancient world. Compare the 'Genius of the Wood' in *Arcades* and *Il Penseroso*, l. 154, and see *Lycidas*, ll. 183–5.

183. *A voice of weeping*: The phrase is Biblical; see Isaiah 45: 19: '. . . the voice of weeping shall be heard no more in [Jerusalem], nor the voice of crying'.

185. *poplar pale*: white-leaved poplar.

188. Compare *Il Penseroso*, ll. 137–8. The Nymphs were 'semi-divine maidens in Greek mythology, expressing the multiform life of Nature' (Wright).

189–96. This stanza represents the native religion of the Romans, characterized by family and tribal gods, the maintenance of whose ritual was essential to social life.

189. The reference is not to the Christian custom of 'consecrating' a burial ground, but to the consecration of certain spots by the Romans, for the cult of their gods.

190. Roman religion was based on the worship of household gods: 'the house was a kind of temple, the dwelling of divine as well as human beings, and the hearth was the centre or altar of this family worship' (Wright).

191. *Lars and Lemures*: Lares (plural of Lar) were spirits which presided over a house or estate, or each of the activities of its owners. The Lemures were the spirits of dead ancestors, ghosts that had to be propitiated.

192. *urns*: the ashes of the dead were kept in clay vessels.

194. *Flamens*: priests, whose duty it was to perform ritual sacrifices.

195. Among other bad omens classical authors refer to the sweating or bleeding of statues of the Gods.

197–228. The description of pagan religions becomes more sinister, with the idols of Syria and Egypt; they are invested with the horror felt for them by the Israelites, and often expressed in the Old Testament.

197. *Peor and Baälim*: Baälim (plural form of Baal) were gods of the Phoenicians and Syrians; their chief male deity was Baal-Peor. See Numbers 25 and 31.

199. Dagon, god of the Philistines, was thrown down on two successive nights in his own temple, when the Philistines placed there 'the ark of God', which they had captured from the Israelites (see 1 Samuel 5: 2–4).

200–1. Ashtaroth was the Hebrew name for the Syrian goddess Astarte, the Queen of Heaven; her symbol was a crescent moon.

203. Hammon (Ammon) was an Egyptian god whose chief shrine was at an oasis in the Libyan desert; he was depicted with the horns of a ram.

204. Thammuz, a beautiful youth loved by Ashtaroth, was killed by a boar while hunting; the myth had a local setting in Syria, where the river Adonis runs down to Byblos from the mountains of Lebanon. The waters of the river turned red every autumn with soil washed down from the mountains by the rains; this was the blood of the wounded Adonis, and a religious festival was held to mourn his death (see Ezekiel 8). The legend and cult (a vegetation myth of the annual death and rebirth of life) were adopted by the Greeks, and the loves of Venus and Adonis passed into European poetry.

Tyrian: Tyre, like Byblos and Sidon, is a city on the coast of Phoenicia.

205. *Moloch*: A god of the Ammonites, who was at times worshipped by the Hebrews, and is often mentioned in the Old Testament. His idol was of brass, with a calf's head; it was hollow and filled with fire, and children were sacrificed to it by being placed on the extended arms of the idol, and so burnt to death. 'And lest their lamentable shrieks should sad the hearts of their parents, the priests of Moloch did deaf their ears with the continual clangs of trumpets and timbrels' (Sandys).

211–12. Many of the Egyptian gods were in animal form, though Isis, Osiris, and Orus were not. Isis was the sister and wife of Osiris; Orus and Anubis were their sons.

213. *Osiris*: 'The legend was that Osiris was a king of Egypt who set forth to subdue the world by the arts of peace; on his return his brother Set (whom the Greeks called Typhon) killed him by shutting him in a chest, which was then thrown into the Nile. Isis wandered in search of her husband and at last found the chest; but Set stole the body, cut it up and scattered the pieces about the earth. Isis recovered the pieces of the body, which with the aid of Anubis were put together and embalmed; then Isis restored life to the body, and Osiris thereafter reigned as king and judge over the dead' (Wright). Osiris became the chief god of the Egyptians, and thus united the powers and attributes of the rest.

214. *Memphian grove*: Osiris was worshipped at a great temple in

Memphis, where he could be seen incarnate in a sacred bull Apis, living in a grassy enclosure.

215. *unshower'd grass*: Egypt is almost rainless.

217. *sacred chest*: When a sacred bull died he was embalmed and buried in a great coffer, which became a shrine, representing the chest containing the embalmed body of Osiris (see l. 213 n.).

219–20. In addition to daily rituals, the priests of Osiris held an annual festival to celebrate the death and resurrection of the god, with processions and music: 'the priests in their holy robes bore the sacred chest, having within it a little gold ark' (Wright).

221–2. Isaiah prophesied that the God of Israel would defeat the gods of Egypt: 'Behold, the LORD rideth upon a swift cloud, and shall come into Egypt: and the idols of Egypt shall be moved at his presence, and the heart of Egypt shall melt in the midst of it . . . and [Egypt] shall be afraid and fear because of the shaking of the hand of the LORD of hosts . . . and the land of Judah shall be a terror unto Egypt . . .' (19). The prophecy was applied later to the coming of Christ.

223. *dusky eyne*: 'one of the symbols of Osiris was a sceptre with an eye in the head, indicating that the god surveys and rules the universe as does the sun' (Wright). His eyes may be dusky because they are deprived of light ('blinded'); but the word gives an image of dark eyes such as Milton and his readers would associate with the Egyptians.

226. *Typhon*: The Greek name for the Egyptian god Set, who was worshipped under the form of a crocodile; in Greek mythology Typhon becomes 'a huge and hideous monster' (Bacon), a many-headed dragon.

227–8. The infant Christ putting the monstrous gods to flight parallels the myth of Hercules in his cradle strangling the serpents.

229–36. Again the new-born Christ is compared to the sun (see ll. 77–84 and 223), with a final appropriate addition to the list of his triumphs; it is based on the popular superstition that ghosts and evil spirits had to disappear at dawn. Marcellus says of the ghost in *Hamlet* (I. i):

It faded on the crowing of the cock.

Christianity taught that evil spirits (i.e. fallen angels) deceived men not only in the form of Greek gods, oriental idols, and so on, but as the fairies and elves of the countryside; the belief in such spirits was indeed a survival of the pagan cult of nymphs, genii, and satyrs.—An otherwise brilliant conclusion is blemished when the rising sun is compared to a sleeper waking, under red curtains of cloud, and with his chin using the eastern sea-line as a pillow: such 'quaintness' shows the influence of the Metaphysical style on a poet whose genius lay in other directions.

232–6. Compare *A Midsummer Night's Dream*, III. ii. 379–82.

fetter'd ghost: Compare *Comus*, ll. 470–5.

236. *night-steeds*: Compare *Comus*, ll. 553–4. The horses may be merely drawing the chariot of Night; or they may be 'nightmares', which were also attributed to evil spirits.

moon-loved maze: 'labyrinths of the woods loved by the huntress Diana, who in association with Hecate was goddess of the fairies' (Wright). See *Comus*, l. 135 n.

241–2. See l. 23 n. and St. Matthew 2: 9: 'and, lo, the star, which they saw in the east, went before them, till it came and stood over where the young child was'. The poem begins with the hour before dawn (ll. 19–21) and concludes with the sun about to rise (ll. 229–31); the reference to the star which leads to Bethlehem in l. 23 is also taken up and expanded to make the conclusion. The star has led us through the poem to the point where it can stand fixed, its task accomplished: everything is ready for us and the world to pay homage to the infant Saviour.

241. *courtly stable*: The stable is now the court where the infant is to be honoured as the new-born King of Heaven and Earth.

On Time and *At a Solemn Music*
(?1632–1633)

In their religious feeling these two pieces prolong the mood of the Nativity Ode; their form develops new effects based on the same principles.

Both poems derive from the Italian madrigal tradition, which was related to *canzone* form; but Milton follows Spenser in the liberties he takes with the Italian rules. Madrigals, like *canzoni*, were constructed out of lines of two lengths (eleven and seven syllables) which become, in English, lines of ten syllables and six. Spenser introduced also Alexandrines into his *Epithalamion* and *Prothalamion*. Milton wished for even more freedom, and added, not only Alexandrines, but lines of eight syllables (in the Nativity Ode) and seven (in these two pieces). Spenser had not observed the strict Italian interweaving of rhymes, Milton disregards it altogether. He concentrates instead on running his sentences over from one line to another, and building up a sustained logical statement; this is another method of making the poem a single verse-paragraph, like a madrigal. The effect, in each poem, is of a fervent burst of feeling, rising to a solemn climax; the conclusions have an almost epigrammatic brilliance, recalling the argument to its starting-point.

Warton comments: 'Milton could not help applying the most solemn and mysterious truths of religion on all subjects and occasions. He has here introduced the beatific vision, and the investiture of the soul with a robe of stars, into an inscription on a clock-case' (the Trinity MS. gives *On Time* the subtitle 'to be set on a clock-case'). Both poems in fact concentrate on the vision of the glory of Heaven which inspired Milton throughout his life. His enthusiasm for the vision of light, music, and blessedness finds expression again and again: most often in a purely religious form, in the great epics and in the Sonnets (IX, XV); but sometimes translated into the mythological terms of an Earthly Paradise or a Golden Age, as in *Comus*, *Lycidas*, and *Paradise Lost*.

L'Allegro and *Il Penseroso*

(?1631–1633)

No precise date can be given for these twin poems; they are generally agreed to reflect Milton's life at Horton, but they also show influences from his Cambridge years. One should not forget that poems of such richness and polish may have taken some time to reach their final form. In any case, 'we may accept them as a psychological picture of his life at Horton, presented under two alternating moods which he calls Melancholy and Mirth' (Wright).

The idea of a pair of linked and contrasted poems, each upholding one way of life as opposed to another, directly recalls the tradition of academic exercises which had come down to the Renaissance from the medieval universities. A student was expected to be able to defend or attack, in Latin, any thesis proposed to him; the debate was both the usual form of examination, and an opportunity for a display of one's abilities. Milton preserved the Latin exercises of this kind that he had to do at Cambridge, one of the earliest being a debate on the relative merits of Night and Day which has affinities with *L'Allegro* and *Il Penseroso*.

We are not therefore to take too seriously the opposition between the Cheerful Man and the Thoughtful Man, or their patrons Mirth and Melancholy. The rhetoric of the opening lines sets the tone of an animated debate in a spirit of enjoyment, and the poet's imagination sympathizes with each way of life in turn. The poems dramatize two aspects of Milton's mind, between which there might be a certain tension, but a tension enhancing life and energy. The poet's task is to re-create in verse the particular objects and experiences which will represent and feed the mood of gaiety or that of thoughtfulness. His guiding light is the Renaissance literary ideal of *decorum*: every detail must be in keeping with the theme and purpose of the poem, and the search for the right note, image, or turn of thought is an inspiring test of skill. Milton seldom so obviously enjoys himself as he seems to do here, even if the final mood is one of spiritual rapture rather than relaxed pleasure. We see the consciousness of a poet in action, his sense of beauty at work, and this gives both poems a sublimated visionary quality which melts into one world the studious and occult concerns, on the one hand, and the country games and court pageants on the other. It is partly this range of sensibility which reminds us of Elizabethan poetry, which Milton has set himself to plunder, in order to enrich his poetic resources.

So the poet remains his serious purposeful self, even amid these pleasures. The framework of the debate shows that polemical, controversial bent of mind which is so important, not only in the prose of his middle years, but in the epics. And the very richness and polish of the style shows that he has applied himself vigorously to the task of every young poet—to master the discipline of his art.

L'Allegro

1–10. The opening lines, as in *Il Penseroso*, are a conjuration, driving away Melancholy and Mirth respectively, as the opposing power to the way of life to be described. The slower rhythm and somewhat exaggerated rhetoric of these introductions contrast with what follows; they are like solemn chords arresting the attention at the beginning of a musical composition. They also provide *within* each poem a contrast echoing that between the poems taken as a pair. The metre alternates five-stress and three-stress lines, of the types combined in the Italian *canzone*; long lines always rhyme with short, not long with long, nor short with short.

2. *Cerberus*: the three-headed dog that guards the threshold of Hades. Melancholy (here, but not in *Il Penseroso*) is the child of Darkness and of the porter of Hell.

3. *Stygian*: from Styx, one of the four rivers of the underworld. The adjective is associated with depth and darkness, but here has also its original meaning of 'hateful'.

10. *Cimmerian*: Homer says the Cimmerians were a people on whom the sun never shone, who lived 'beyond the Ocean stream'.

11–40. In both poems Milton moves towards the catalogue of pleasures by way of an invocation to the power, or goddess, which can offer them. The invocation here falls into two parts, the genealogy of the goddess and the description of her followers and companions (25–36). In *Il Penseroso* these two elements recur (22–30 and 45–55), but they are merged into descriptions of Melancholy's appearance (13–21) and behaviour (31–44). The method of personifying a mood or passion, and listing its accompanying experiences or actions as personifications, came down from Latin poetry, through medieval allegory, to Spenser and Milton; see e.g. *Faerie Queene*, III. xii (the Masque of Cupid), and the Mutabilitie Cantos, vii.

12. *Euphrosyne*: Blitheness, one of the three Graces: the others were Aglaia and Thalia; they are all goddesses of festivity, and friends of the Muses.

14–17. Venus, the goddess of love, and Bacchus, the god of wine, were only one couple suggested as parents of the Graces (cf. Spenser, *Faerie Queene*, VI. x. 22); Milton in the next lines invents another genealogy. Bacchus usually wears a crown of ivy; see *Comus*, l. 55.

19. Zephyr is the west wind, Aurora the dawn. For the west wind and spring, see also Sonnet XVI, l. 6.

29. Hebe is the goddess of youth, and cupbearer to the Gods.

36. Mountains are associated with freedom, those dwelling among them being difficult to conquer or control.

41–150. The first stretches of the poem (rather less than a third in all) have been preliminaries to the catalogue of pleasures, which now begins. These are divided into (i) country pleasures (41–116) and (ii) town pleasures (117–34), followed by a crowning passage in praise of music (135–50). This reflects back on the whole way of life described in the poem; for music and poetry are identified in Orpheus (145–50), and Milton really celebrates the vision of life of a young poet, as he knows it from experience.

41. *To hear*: The 'I' of the poem, the poet, is to live with Mirth, to hear the lark, 'to come in spite of sorrow' (l. 45) and greet the day, as he is to experience the other delights that follow. 'There are three distinct statements dependent on "Mirth admit me of thy crew", which are separated by semicolons and are each introduced by an infinitive: "To live with her . . .", "To hear the lark . . .", "Then to come . . ." ' (Wright).

41–116. The country pleasures are framed and ordered by the phases of a day, from dawn to midnight. But the day includes both work (63–8) and holiday (91–8), and various seasons (68, 87–90).

48. *eglantine*: strictly the same as 'sweet-briar', but 'twisted' indicates a climbing plant like the honeysuckle.

49–56. A time clause ('While . . . before') is followed by a present participle ('listening'), which serves for a sentence with 'I' as subject. This is echoed by another participle ('walking'), followed by another time clause ('While . . . dale'). Milton's use of syntax throughout is skilful and varied, but logically loose: it succeeds because of the swift dancing rhythm and regular rhyme.

57. *not unseen*: Cf. *Il Penseroso*, l. 65. L'Allegro does not avoid company, Il Penseroso does.

69–70. New sources of pleasure are suddenly opened, with a more direct and energetic form of statement, and a variation of rhythm (with the 'feminine' rhymes). A wide landscape is projected, with mountains, rivers, meadows, woods, castles, and cottages, leading again to country work and pastimes.

83. *Corydon and Thyrsis*: Stock names for shepherds or country-men in pastoral poetry; Phillis (l. 86) and Thestylis (l. 88) are feminine equivalents. Virgil echoed Theocritus in using such names: Milton echoes both. Completely English rustic life ('cottage chimney', 'oaks', 'dinner') is decorated with classical references, which add sonority and an aura of timelessness.

100–16. The countryfolk's day ends with ale, supper, and stories told round the fire; the season is undefined, but such 'old wives' tales' were also called 'winter's tales'. The allusions to fairies and goblins recall Shakespeare's *Midsummer Night's Dream*.

102. *fairy Mab*: Cf. Queen Mab in *Romeo and Juliet*, I. iv. 54–95. The fairies helped or hindered in dairy-work, and were propitiated by curds or cream left to be eaten during the night (l. 106).

103. *pinch'd and pull'd*: Fairies showed their disapproval (of laziness or neglect) in this way. See *Merry Wives of Windsor*, v. v.

104. *Friar's Lantern*: A light which misled countrymen or travellers at night; like the 'will-o'-the-wisp', it was supposed to be the work of a mischievous or spiteful spirit.

105. *drudging goblin*: Hobgoblin, Shakespeare's Puck or Robin Goodfellow, who was full of pranks, but would also do heavy work if well treated. Burton in *The Anatomy of Melancholy* (i, Sec. 2. 1. 2) mentions 'hobgoblins, and Robin Goodfellows, that would in those superstitious times grind corn for a mess of milk, cut wood, or do any manner of drudgery work'.

117–34. The transition to town pleasures is made by a contrast between village life, and the high buildings and crowds of cities. There is the outline of a day here too, passing from daylight tourna-ments to wedding feasts by artificial light, and the theatre. Yet even here a mood of reverie is introduced, as if the poet is evoking even these urban festivities in rural solitude (129–30).

123. *wit or arms*: Tournaments had survived the Middle Ages as a form of court entertainment, a display of horsemanship and skill in handling weapons. But such exercises of chivalry were gradually

absorbed into masques and pageants, dramatic or poetic inventions. 'Wit' was thus also displayed, in complimentary verse or prose speeches, in allegory, and in riddling 'impreses', heraldic devices with mottoes.

126. *Hymen*: god of marriage, who would appear in a wedding masque dressed in a yellow robe and holding a torch.

130. Cf. Nativity Ode, l. 184.

132. *Jonson's learnèd sock*: Ben Jonson (1572–1637), the most learned of the Elizabethan dramatists, was most successful in comedy. The 'sock' was a light shoe (*soccus*) worn by Greek and Roman comic actors, and thus became an emblem for comic drama.

133. *Fancy's*: imagination's. See *Comus*, l. 548.

134. *native wood-notes wild*: Milton's mastery of phrase here summarizes what was to be the general view of Shakespeare's genius until the birth of a new school of criticism in Germany and England in the late eighteenth and early nineteenth centuries; Shakespeare was a 'natural', untutored poet, who 'wanted art' (Ben Jonson). 'Native' alludes to Shakespeare's country origins in Warwickshire.

136. *Lydian*: The Lydian mode was used for sweet and tender music by the Greeks, who thought of it as somewhat effeminate. The other two modes of Greek music were the Dorian and the Phrygian, the former solemn, the latter warlike.

143–4. J. B. Leishman calls this 'a Platonic conceit, . . . where the soul of harmony is conceived of as a kind of sleeping beauty, . . . awakened into life, by the singer and the instruments'.[1]

145–50. For Milton Orpheus is the archetypal poet-musician; see *Il Penseroso*, ll. 105–8; *Lycidas*, ll. 58–63; *Paradise Lost*, VII, ll. 32–8. The song of Orpheus had power over wild beasts, and even trees and rocks. When his wife Eurydice died he went down into Hades and by his music so charmed Persephone and Pluto, the King of the underworld, that he was given permission to take Eurydice back to life, on condition that, as they ascended to daylight, he leading and she behind, he would not look back to see if she was following. But Orpheus turned his head, and Eurydice had to go back for ever.

[1] 'L'Allegro and Il Penseroso in their Relation to Seventeenth Century Poetry', *Essays and Studies 1951.*

148. *Elysian*: paradisal. Elysium was the abode of the happy dead in Greek religion.

151–2. The abrupt concluding couplet looks back to ll. 39–40. See *Il Penseroso*, ll. 175–6. Milton has adapted the conclusion of Marlowe's song, *The Passionate Shepherd to his Love*:

> If these delights thy mind may move,
> Then live with me, and be my love.

Il Penseroso

1–10. See *L'Allegro*, ll. 1–10 n.

10 *Morpheus*: god of dreams, the son of Sleep.

11–60. Cf. *L'Allegro*, ll. 11–40. The invocation, description, genealogy, and companions of Melancholy occupy more space than those of Mirth, and the transition to the pleasures she offers is not so explicit. Milton is following a pattern, but lets the details develop freely. Thus Silence is the last of Melancholy's followers to be listed; she suggests the silence surrounding the nightingale's song; and the nightingale leads to the poet listening, and his wanderings in the countryside at night.

15–21. Dürer's engraving of Melencolia gives her a dusky face; Milton's allusions show that he wishes her to have an African complexion. The long Greek, medieval, and Renaissance tradition behind Dürer's and Milton's conception is expounded by E. Panofsky, R. Klibansky, and others, in *Saturn and Melancholy* (London, 1964).

17. *Prince Memnon's sister*: Memnon, a prince of Ethiopia, fought with the Trojans against the Greeks; Homer calls him the handsomest of men. Later writers said he had a sister, Hemera, who might be presumed to be equally beautiful.

19–21. The 'Ethiop queen' is Cassiope, who was transformed into the constellation of Cassiopeia (hence 'starr'd'). She was the wife of Cepheus, King of Ethiopia, and offended the Nereids (sea-nymphs) by boasting, not of her own beauty, as Milton says, but of her daughter Andromeda's. The Nereids sent a flood and a sea-monster to punish Ethiopia, and demanded that Andromeda be sacrificed to the monster. Andromeda was rescued by Perseus, and became a constellation, like her mother.

23. *Vesta*: the Roman goddess of the hearth. She was worshipped

under the symbol of an eternal fire (the flames of which would be her 'bright hair') tended by her priestesses, the vestal virgins. By making her the mother of Melancholy Milton suggests study or thought indoors (see ll. 77–84).

24. *Saturn*: Saturn, the youngest of the Titans, was the father of the Olympians and the founder of civilization. In astrology he was identified with the planet Saturn, which was farthest from the earth and slowest in its movement, and therefore considered solitary and gloomy. Those born under Saturn's influence were melancholy in temperament ('saturnine').

25–30. 'Saturn's reign' was a golden age, when men lived without the restraints of law, and the earth yielded crops without changes of season (see Nativity Ode, l. 135). Saturn's seat of power was Mount Ida in Crete; when he was overthrown by his son Jove, the abode of the Gods became Mount Olympus.

43. *leaden*: 'The theory of astrology was that, the universe being one, the heavenly bodies must exercise a constant influence on earthly conditions; . . . Colours, metals, stones, plants, and animal and human life in all its aspects were assigned to their respective planets and stars. Thus Saturn was associated with the colour grey, the metal lead, and so on, as well as with the melancholy temperament' (Wright).

46. Temperance in diet frees the mind from earthly desires and gives it insight into poetry and spiritual realities.

47–8. See *Lycidas*, ll. 15–16.

52–4. The throne of God with fiery wheels, guided by Cherubim, comes from the vision of Ezekiel (chap. 10). 'Cherubim, signifying "fulness of knowledge", were those angels who lived in the contemplation of God, of the divine beauty and wisdom' (Wright). 'Milton ventures to *name* one of the Cherubs in Ezekiel' (Masson). Cf. *At a Solemn Music*, ll. 10–13.

56. *Philomel*: the nightingale.

59. *Cynthia*: the moon-goddess. The dragons drawing her chariot probably derive from the other aspect of the triple moon-goddess, Hecate, who presided over witchcraft. Cf. *Comus*, l. 135.

74. *curfew*: 'The curfew bell was rung in the Middle Ages to announce the time for extinguishing all fires' (Wright).

63–154. Il Penseroso's night (63–121), followed by his day (122–54), corresponds to L'Allegro's day followed by his night (see *L'Allegro*, Commentary). It begins with the nightingale's song at evening (cf. Sonnet I, ll. 1–2), continues with the moon riding high, and takes us indoors late at night (78–84); but it is spent chiefly in midnight study ranging from Platonic philosophy and astrology to Greek tragedy, Greek epic, medieval romance, and allegory (85–120). The story-telling, poetry, and drama, which in *L'Allegro* were a part of social life (101–34), are here enjoyed in study and solitude.

87. *the Bear*: the constellation of the Great Bear.

88–96. The contemplative man prefers to take his science in an occult form, choosing the Neo-Platonic and Hermetic philosophy of the Renaissance, which had largely displaced the Aristotelian scholasticism of the Middle Ages. For an account of Renaissance Platonism see Appendix I.

88. *thrice-great Hermes*: Hermes Trismegistus, the name given by Neo-Platonists of the late classical period to a legendary religious philosopher, supposed to be the author or original teacher of magic, alchemical and mystical doctrines. See Appendix I.

89. *Plato*: See Appendix I.

99–102. *Thebes*: the city ruled by Oedipus, and the scene of tragedies by Aeschylus and Sophocles. *Pelops' line*: Pelops was the ancestor of Agamemnon, Orestes, Iphigenia, and Electra, all of whom are the subjects of surviving Greek tragedies. *The tale of Troy*: The fall of Troy, and the fate of the Trojan women, were made the basis of several plays by Euripides.

101–2. Milton did not find much to admire in tragic drama after the Greeks. He disapproved of Elizabethan tragedy for its mixture of 'comic stuff with tragic sadness and gravity' (see the preface to *Samson Agonistes*).

102. *buskin'd stage*: As the 'sock' was the emblem of comedy (see *L'Allegro*, l. 132), the buskin was that of tragedy; it was a high boot worn by Greek tragic actors to increase their stature.

103–20. The poetry evoked here is all either legendary, lost, unfinished, or mysterious; the contemplative man is absorbed in speculation or unravelling a hidden meaning.

104. *Musaeus*: a mythical Greek poet, sometimes said to be the son of Orpheus.

105. *Orpheus*: See *L'Allegro*, ll. 145–50.

109–15. The references are to *The Squire's Tale*, which Chaucer left unfinished. Cambuscan is a Tartar king, who has three children, Algarsyf, Cambal, and Canace. Canace's lover gave her a magic ring and mirror, and offered her father a brazen horse that could carry its rider any distance within twenty-four hours.

116–20. Spenser's *Faerie Queene*, which combines chivalric romance with moral allegory, is probably the poem Milton means us to think of first; but he also admired Ariosto and Tasso, and felt the appeal of earlier medieval romances.

122–30. Day dawns in rain and cloud, not in the fine weather of *L'Allegro* (44–62). As the sun rises higher, Il Penseroso takes refuge in shadowy woods, where he can feel the presence of nature spirits, and drowse (he has been awake all night). In his sleep he will have a 'mysterious dream', which will give him further matter for thought. When he wakes, it will be to the sound of supernatural music.

124. *Attic boy*: Cephalus, whose grandfather Cecrops was King of Attica, was loved by Eos, the dawn-goddess, who first saw him out hunting.

134. *Sylvan*: Roman god of woods and trees.

137–8. Cf. Nativity Ode, ll. 181–8 n.

155–74. The transition to music has been made in l. 151, but the symmetry with *L'Allegro* (135–50) demands a eulogy of sacred music. This leads naturally to the religious solitary, the hermit, and to his old age, when a lifetime of contemplation will be rewarded by the vision of heavenly truth.

171–2. See l. 43 n., and Appendix I.

175–6. Cf. *L'Allegro*, ll. 151–2.

Arcades and *Comus*

(?1633 and 1634)

The Court Masque

That Milton appreciated the brilliance and charm of court pageantry is clear from *L'Allegro* (ll. 120–30). He may have been led to try his own hand at it by his love of music, the basis of his friendship with the composer Henry Lawes (see Sonnet VIII). They probably became acquainted through the Milton family's interest in music. Lawes was attached to the household of John Egerton, Earl of Bridgewater, as tutor to the children, and as such was to act the part of the Attendant Spirit in *Comus* (and probably the Genius of the Wood in *Arcades*). Lawes must have asked his young friend to contribute some verses to the entertainment to be given at Harefield in honour of the Dowager Countess of Derby, by members of her family; these included the young Egertons, whose father was stepson of the Dowager. *Arcades* no doubt led to the more ambitious *Comus*, designed for the installation of Lord Bridgewater as Lord President of Wales in 1634.

The first piece was slight, only 'part of an entertainment'; the second was rounded out with a plot, and was much more substantial, even in the acting version. Both come towards the end of a long tradition of such entertainments, which in the previous forty years had risen to a new splendour and literary prestige.

The masque was introduced into England from Italy in the sixteenth century. Its name and its central feature derived from an Italian custom which we see in *Romeo and Juliet*: a group of masked persons would visit a dance at Court or in a private house, invited or uninvited, mingle with the guests, and reveal their identity as the night wore on. In England the masque took its place among other court spectacles such as tournaments, pageants, and interludes. Music, dance, and song, the essential elements, were often framed in a slight dramatic action or anecdote. Under Queen Elizabeth the masque became a recognized means of complimenting the sovereign, and many poets seized the opportunities it offered. Great nobles receiving the Queen would mount such little pageants on their country estates, their great houses being like local 'Courts'; but the grandest spectacles would be at Whitehall or in the Inns of Court. The Court masque reached its height, both theatrical and poetical, under

James I, whose court was more extravagant and ostentatious than Elizabeth's; it was James's Poet Laureate, Ben Jonson, who between about 1605 and 1630 gave the form a new scope and dignity, loading his masques with classical learning, fantasy, humour, and moral allegories of the noble life.

Even in its ordered and artistic glory under the Stuarts, the Court masque was a mixed form, in which the contributions of the poet, the stage designer, and the musician might struggle for dominance. Ben Jonson had as collaborator Inigo Jones, whose genius for architecture and machinery produced brilliant results; but Jonson became jealous, and they quarrelled. The increased use of theatrical machines favoured plots involving magic or the supernatural, such as we find in *The Tempest* and other late plays by Shakespeare; and this tendency may have influenced Milton's choice of theme in *Comus*, though the stage effects there were limited by its being presented at Ludlow.

Jonson's methods of construction fixed a common form for the majority of Jacobean and Caroline masques, which has been summarized by B. A. Wright:

> In construction the fully developed masque consists of two main parts, the antimasque and the masque proper. First the action and purport of the piece, including its complimentary significance, was explained in a prologue; the prologue soon developed into a dramatic scene between two or more characters, and out of this in turn developed the antimasque. The antimasque was a preliminary masque serving as a contrast or foil to the main masque; and since the latter was an expression of heroic virtue and beauty, the antimasque was realistic, ribald, and grotesque. For instance, Jonson's 'Masque of Queens,' in which the Queen and some of her ladies took part, celebrates 'honourable and true Fame, bred out of Virtue'; the antimasque accordingly presents twelve witches 'sustaining the persons of Ignorance, Suspicion, Credulity, etc., the opposites of good fame,' who appear in an opening scene similar to that in the Fourth Act of 'Macbeth', and perform grotesque dances 'full of preposterous change and gesticulation.' During this preliminary part of the entertainment, whatever form it took, the masquers proper were concealed within the scene, and it was the dramatist's and producer's principal care to render their first appearance as effective as possible; for this was the

dramatic climax of the show. At the appropriate moment they were revealed either by a transformation scene or by a part of the scene opening in the form of a shell or a cave, or some such device. They were then welcomed in speech or song by the other characters; after which they moved in procession down from the stage to the dancing floor in the middle of the hall and performed their three or four sets of formal courtly dances. The dances were interspersed with songs which served both to interpret their dramatic significance and to give the dancers a breathing space; and between the second and third set usually came the ordinary social dances in which the masquers chose partners from the audience. After their final dance the masquers withdrew to the stage and the play concluded with a final song.[1]

Arcades

(? 1633)

Arcades represents the simplest kind of masque, a country version of those court entertainments which enacted a compliment (see *L'Allegro*, ll. 119–24). Some younger members of a noble family dress up as nymphs and shepherds; they are supposed to have come from Arcadia, led by the fame of a great lady (who is in real life the head of their family). They find her enthroned in her little kingdom, that is, her country estate; the scene could be in a Great Hall, or in the park.

The image of royal power seated in state and receiving vows of allegiance is frequent in Milton's verse, from the Nativity Ode to the descriptions of God and Satan in *Paradise Lost*, and God in Sonnet XV.

The action is in four phases, marked by three songs and a speech:

(i) The Arcadians approach and sing, rejoicing in the success of their search for the goddess-queen, and praising her.

(ii) Preparing to pay homage, they are interrupted by a local deity, who identifies them (for the benefit of the audience) and offers to help them. He then identifies himself, and describes his functions: when he is not cherishing the wood, he contemplates the

[1] *Shorter Poems of John Milton,* ed. B. A. Wright (London, 1938), pp. 140–1.

heavens. He offers to echo the music of the spheres in his singing and playing, as he leads them towards the throne.

(iii) The local spirit exhorts the Arcadians, in a song, to follow him.

(iv) They dance in homage before the goddess enthroned. The concluding song invites them to dance no longer in Arcadia, but in England, and acts as a dismissal.

The occasion of *Arcades* gave Milton no scope for deep feeling, which is roused in him only by a powerful moral idea. His best poems are nearly always a celebration of a *way of life*. Here he can be said to pay tribute to the aristocratic way of life, in its exercise of power and virtue; but he does so only by implication, surrounding the subject with images of divine power, pastoral innocence, and natural and cosmic order. The lyrics are perfect in tone, in singing quality, and in their evocation of English and Greek landscapes. But the speech by the Genius is not very well contrived (though essential as explanation and compliment): the strangers have already found the goddess, they do not need help. Milton gives it force and brilliance, notably by ingenious syntax; and raises its interest by introducing favourite themes—the nature spirits fostering fertility, and the music of the spheres.

Arcades lacks a vital centre, but the songs show Milton outdoing Ben Jonson and other Elizabethans in writing verse of concentrated beauty for musical settings.

(Subtitle and Stage Direction)

Countess Dowager of Derby: The countess was at least seventy years of age, and the head of a large family which included her own children by her first husband, the children of her second husband, and her grandchildren. She was by birth a Spencer (honoured as Amaryllis by Spenser in *Colin Clout's Come Home Again*), and had as her first husband Lord Strange, patron of poets and actors, who became the fifth Earl of Derby and died in 1594. In 1600 Lady Derby married Sir Thomas Egerton, who later became Lord Chancellor Baron Ellesmere, and finally Viscount Brackley before his death in 1617. His widow retained her old title of Countess of Derby. Her daughter had married Sir John Egerton, the son of her second husband by his former marriage; he became Earl of Bridgewater and was appointed Lord President of the Council of Wales in 1631.

Harefield: A family estate where the countess continued to live after the death of Lord Brackley; it is about twelve miles from Horton.

some noble persons of her family: These would presumably be for the most part her grandchildren, and include the three Egerton children, Lady Alice, Lord Brackley, and Thomas Egerton, who later acted in *Comus*.

20–1. Both deities are mother-goddesses. *Latona* is the Latin name for the Greek Leto, mother of Apollo and Diana, her children by Zeus. Persecuted by Hera (Juno), the wife of Zeus, she wandered about until she gave birth to her twins on the island of Ortygia (see Sonnet VII, l. 6). *Tow'rèd Cybele* was an Asiatic goddess, called Mother of the Gods, and identified by the Greeks with Rhea. Cybele was regarded as the mother of both nature and civilization, and worshipped as the founder of cities; hence she was represented in art with a diadem of towers.

22. *a hundred gods*: i.e. the noble descendants of the Dowager Countess.

23. 'Juno would not dare to compete with her on equal terms (lay aside her divinity).' As the wife of Jupiter, Juno was Queen of the Gods.

26–7. 'Gentle swains' is a contradiction in terms (oxymoron), which is immediately explained by the statement that the Genius has penetrated their disguise.

28. *Arcady*: In ancient Greece Arcadia was a state in the Peloponnese, shut off by mountain barriers, and retaining a primitive simplicity of life. In sixteenth-century Renaissance literature it became the setting of pastoral romance and poetry, an imaginary country where shepherds and nymphs lived almost as innocently and happily as in the Age of Gold.

29–31. *that renownèd flood . . . Alpheus . . . Arethuse*: The chief river of Arcadia and the Peloponnese was the Alpheus, which ran underground for part of its course. Its river-god was originally a hunter, who fell in love with a nymph Arethusa, as she was bathing in the river. She fled his advances, and was changed into a fountain by the goddess of chastity, Diana; sinking underground, her waters rose again at Ortygia in Sicily. But Alpheus, still pursuing her, also changed into a river, also flowed under the sea to Sicily, and there was united with Arethusa. See *Lycidas*, l. 133.

33. *silver-buskin'd*: The buskin was a boot worn by huntsmen; the masquers here would wear it as followers of Diana, the chaste huntress. Cf. *Il Penseroso*, l. 102 n.

48–53. Cf. *Comus*, ll. 640, 843–6, and *Lycidas*, ll. 44–5, 126–7.

63–73. A summary of 'the "Vision of Er" at the close of Plato's "Republic", in which Socrates describes in a myth the judgment of souls in the other world. The souls come to a place where they see the Spindle of Necessity (i.e. the law of the universe), made of adamant, which holds the universe together and by which its revolutions are produced and maintained; it is driven as an axis through the centre of the earth and the eight spheres, and rests in the lap of Necessity. On each of the spheres sits a siren who utters one note at one pitch, the eight notes making together the harmony of the octave. Seated at equal distances about Necessity are the Fates, Lachesis and Clotho and Atropos, the daughters of Necessity; Lachesis sings of the past, Clotho of the present, and Atropos of the future, and it is they who turn the Spindle of Necessity' (Wright).

64. *nine . . . spheres*: See Appendix I.

65. The shears were in fact held only by Atropos, who cut the thread of life which her sisters spun and drew out. Cf. *Lycidas*, ll. 75–6.

79. *lesser gods*; i.e. spirits or local divinities. See Nativity Ode, ll. 181–8.

97–102. The names are those of rivers and mountains in Arcadia. The Ladon was a tributary of the Alpheus, often called 'sandy' in poetry. Lycaeus, Cyllene, and Maenalus are Arcadian mountains, Erymanthus is the name of both a mountain and a river.

106–7. The places mentioned in this song are typical haunts of Pan, the Arcadian god of hills and woods. Syrinx was the daughter of the river-god Ladon; Pan fell in love with her, and pursued her on the banks of the river, but she was changed by her sister-nymphs into a reed. From this Pan cut a pipe, known as a Syrinx. Cf. Nativity Ode, l. 89, and *Comus*, l. 176.

Comus

(1634)

Comus follows the Jonsonian pattern for a Court masque in many features, while aiming at a rather different result—a dramatic poem on a philosophical theme.

The poem can be divided into five sections:

(i) The Prologue (1–92), which leads directly into the action. The Attendant Spirit states the theme in general terms—the intervention of heavenly powers to help men in their struggle with evil (1–17; note that the concluding couplet (1022–3) reaffirms the theme); and explains that this is his task, and in what circumstances. The Lord President's children are on their way to join him, and must pass through the wood, where they are in danger from an enchanter (18–82). The action then begins to move (82–92).

(ii) In the Antimasque (93–169), Comus enters and revels with his crew; they hide at the approach of the Lady. She enters, tells us she is lost, and sings, hoping to be heard by her Brothers (170–243). Comus comes forward, and she accepts his offer to lead her to safety (244–340).

(iii) The Two Brothers discuss their sister's danger. The Attendant Spirit, disguised as a shepherd, comes to tell them that she is in the hands of the enchanter. He advises them how to rescue her, and leads them off to do so (331–658).

(iv) Comus has brought the Lady to his palace, and tempts her with a magic potion, which she refuses. As he is about to force it on her, the Brothers rush in and drive him and his followers away; but the Lady is seated in an enchanted chair, and cannot be released until the Attendant Spirit has summoned the local river-goddess, Sabrina, to dissolve the spell. The Attendant Spirit offers to guide the children to their father's residence (659–957).

(v) The scene changes to Ludlow, where the countryfolk dance in honour of the Lord President's installation. The Spirit leads in the Lady and her Brothers, and presents them to their parents in two songs; these are followed by a general dance. The Attendant Spirit speaks an Epilogue.

We see that Milton has provided the expected compliments, an antimasque, songs and changes of scene, effects depending on stage machinery, and dances and songs bringing together the actors and audience at the end. But the poetry has grown at the expense of the theatrical and musical components, because the poet's purpose is to dramatize a debate on a moral choice—how to live. The masque in his hands has become a coherent form of poetic drama, but it is a form that does not require much plot-interest, or characterization, or realistic detail. The characters are simple, and so are their relationships with one another. Their speeches are often long, closely argued, and richly ornamented. Their actions are circumscribed by supernatural or magic powers (as in Shakespeare's *Tempest*, but more appropriately here).

The unrealities and improbabilities of the action (e.g. the vague ness about the young people's travel arrangements, and why the Brothers left the Lady alone) are in keeping with the atmosphere of a fairy-tale and its moral. The masque conventions encourage make-believe: the occasion of the performance is the Lord President's installation, and this is referred to in the Prologue and at the end. The audience watches the drama, and takes part in it; having been spectators of the installation, they join in the conclusion of the masque, just as the children emerge from the masque and join their parents.

If we accept that *Comus* is in a special dramatic form, limited by conventions, we are free to admire the efficiency with which Milton uses it. A dramatic logic and intelligence are at work throughout, though some passages have been considered weak. The climax of the action is the Lady's temptation by Comus, and his speeches make it also a climax in the philosophical debate, since he states the case for the life of pleasure. The Lady's replies have been compared to their disadvantage with the eloquence of Comus (sometimes to arrive at the conclusion that Milton is really on the side of the tempter). But Milton shows aesthetic and social tact in not making the Lady argue at length or vociferously; and he manages this by arranging for the full philosophic statement of her position to be given earlier, and not by herself. She does indeed appeal to the rational discipline of Temperance and 'the sage and serious doctrine of Virginity'; but their beauty and power have already been expounded fully by her Brother in the preceding scene (359–475). Her comparative reticence is also justified by her confidence in the protection of Heaven, which has also been asserted by the Elder Brother, and is indeed written into the drama from its opening lines.

The mission of the Attendant Spirit to help the young people pro-
vides evidence in advance, of the truth of what the Elder Brother
claims and the Lady believes (210–20).[1]

So the dramatic interest consists in little more than following the
enactment of what we have been led to expect. If we are sometimes
reminded of the simplicities of old-fashioned pantomime, that is not
inappropriate. What matters is the journey of the innocent through
the dark wood of life, its trials and dangers, the help of good
spirits, God helping those who help themselves. Dr. Johnson was
amused by the lack of urgency in the dialogue between the Brothers
(though even here the fears of the younger are a vivid reminder of
the Lady's plight, and the Elder Brother's speeches make the scene
the living *moral* centre of the poem). The arrival of the Brothers just
as Comus offers the Lady violence is not a clumsy use of coincidence:
it is a demonstration of Providence intervening to save virtue—what
we have been promised, what we expect, and what we have just
been reminded of by the Lady and by Comus himself (793–801).
The invocation and ready response of Sabrina give another visible
form to the frustration of evil by supernatural powers; and the
Epilogue clinches the moral (1021–2).

The moral teaching of Comus is related clearly to Milton's
religion, his philosophical ideas, and his way of life at this time.
Christian values are not expressed directly, but in the modes of
Renaissance allegory and Platonic philosophy. The Prologue refers
to Plato's doctrine of virtue as founded on reason and knowledge.
Plato's theory of the soul is preached by the Elder Brother in his
eulogy of wisdom and of chastity as an obvious and vital form of
virtue (373–85 and 453–75). The soul, which is immortal, can be
contaminated, and may be utterly degraded, by material desires and
their satisfactions; but if it is true to itself and resists, it can triumph
and rise to Heaven (970–5 and 1003–23).

Chastity, the particular virtue illustrated in *Comus*, had great
importance in Plato's thought, as a means of liberating the soul from
attachment to earthly things. But as Milton presents it, the emphasis
falls on virginity, not on chastity in the wider sense, and this is more
characteristic of the Christian tradition. Virginity as a means to, and
as a mark of, sanctity was always extolled by Catholic Christianity.
The Protestant Reformation rejected it as an ideal, together with

[1] See also ll. 221–5 n. and ll. 230–1 n.

the medieval conception of the religious life; but the Reformers could not and did not deny the value of chastity as a practical virtue, requiring virginity before marriage and fidelity after it.

Milton would find in Spenser's *Faerie Queene* many beautiful episodes which are designed to praise both virginity and married chastity, for in Elizabethan England the cult of the Virgin Queen had given the medieval sentiment a new, if rather artificial, lease of life. But Milton's temperament, his upbringing, and his poetic vocation combined to give the ideal a quite personal significance for him in his youth. A certain pride and fastidiousness of nature, and a sensitive and eager response to physical beauty, are joined to a diffidence arising perhaps from his studious way of life, perhaps from an instinct that he is not yet ready for adult responsibilities. But he certainly does not accept virginity as an end in itself, though he surrounds it with the glamour and charm it had in medieval romance and in Spenser. He has the Elizabethan poetic feeling for the old religion, though his moral philosophy belongs to the new: sexual purity is not an end in itself, but a preparation for active adult life. *Comus* was written for the children of a noble family, and designed as an emblem of their education for life in the great world, with its dangers and responsibilities.

Finally, let us remember that poetry is not philosophy or theology, but an art transcending and reconciling (or giving the illusion of reconciling) the conflicts and contradictions of real life. In *Comus* sensuous poetry is used to celebrate the victory over sensuality, Platonic asceticism is married to Christian faith. Moral purity for Milton is a form of beauty, and he wants it to live in harmony with that love of physical beauty, in man and nature, which the poetry everywhere reveals. Unlike Plato's philosophy, Christianity hopes for the salvation of both body and soul; if the body is disciplined, it is in order that it may be redeemed and glorified. Milton uses his art to create a vision of life in which goodness and beauty are fused into one.

The Copy of a Letter written by Sir Henry Wotton

Sir Henry Wotton (1568–1639) wrote to Milton from Eton, where he had been Provost since his retirement from diplomacy. He had been English Ambassador in Venice for many years, was intelligent, cultivated, and witty, a friend of Donne and of many other outstanding men of his time.

32 *Mr H.*: probably John Hales (1584–1656), a Fellow of Merton College and later of Eton. He was much liked by poets and men of letters, who valued his learning and critical judgement.

51. *Mr R.*: John Rouse, Librarian of the Bodleian in Oxford.

the late R.'s Poems: Thomas Randolph's poems, which were printed at Oxford in 1638, may be meant. No copy has been found which incorporates the 1637 edition of *Comus*.

58–9. *Mr. M. B.*: Michael Branthwaite, an English agent at Paris.

60. *Lord S.*: the son of Lord Scudamore, who represented Charles I in Paris.

80–1. *i pensieri stretti*: Wotton may have been hinting that Milton would give offence by speaking freely against the Catholic Church. If so, the hint was not taken; Milton's Italian friends seem to have admired everything about him except his criticisms of their religion.

(Stage Direction)

a wild wood: This would be a painted scene in the hall of Ludlow Castle, not a real wood as it might be in *Arcades*. The setting is appropriate for a story of trial or temptation; Dante finds himself in 'a dark wood' at the beginning of the *Divine Comedy*.

Attendant Spirit: In both surviving manuscripts the description is 'A Guardian Spirit, or Daemon'. In Greek and Roman religion every individual had a daemon or genius, which guided his life, like the guardian angel of Christian belief. Milton wished his spiritual universe to recall classical philosophy rather than medieval religion. The part was acted by Henry Lawes, whose name does not appear in the published list of actors.

descends: In the performance the Attendant Spirit entered with a song beginning 'From the Heavens now I fly', and may have come down in flight by means of machinery. In the printed version the song is at the end, where it forms the Epilogue (ll. 976–1023); it was probably written originally for that purpose.

1. *Jove's court*: Jupiter held court on Mount Olympus, whose summit rose above the clouds.

18, 20. Neptune, god of the sea, was the brother of Jupiter ('high Jove') and Pluto ('nether Jove'), who ruled the sky and the underworld respectively. After they had overthrown their father Saturn, the three brothers divided the universe among them by casting lots.

27. *tridents*: The trident was the sceptre of Neptune.

46–9. Bacchus was carried off to sea by some Italian sailors, who plotted to sell him as a slave; the god escaped by driving them to throw themselves overboard in a frenzy, when they were transformed into dolphins.

the Tyrrhene sea: the sea off the coast of Tuscany.

50–4. Homer describes Circe as the daughter of the Sun, an enchantress living on the island of Aeaea, where she was visited by Odysseus and his companions in their wanderings. Her island was full of tame lions and wolves, and she transformed half Odysseus' men into swine.

57. Comus was like the god of wine, in his feasting and intemperance, but more like his mother Circe in his sorceries.

58. *Comus*: His name comes from a Greek word for 'revelry', and Ben Jonson had depicted him as a gluttonous god of feasts (in *Pleasure Reconciled to Virtue*, 1618). By making Circe his mother, Milton attributed to Comus sinister beauty and witchcraft as well as revelry.

60. *Celtic and Iberian fields*: The plains of France and Spain, both great wine-growing countries.

68–77. The story of Circe in Homer had been elaborated by Renaissance writers, and given the moral Milton uses. Homer's Circe transforms her victims into swine by mixing drugs with their food. Milton increases the types of animals, though in the *Odyssey* it is not certain that those other than hogs were not merely wild beasts tamed. In France in 1582 Beaujoyeulx used the myth in a brilliant court-entertainment, the *Ballet Comique de la Reine*; this was plagiarized by Inigo Jones in *Tempe Restor'd*, presented at Whitehall in 1631.

83. Iris was the goddess of the rainbow, the messenger of the gods, one of the Oceanides.

97. *Atlantic stream*: another name for the Ocean Stream which the Greeks thought encircled the earth. See l. 868 n.

129–36 Cotytto was a Thracian goddess whose festival, held by night, was notorious for its licentiousness. It is Milton's invention to have her escorted by the witch Hecate. As a goddess of the under-world, Hecate was closely akin to Proserpina; as a goddess of night, she was associated with Diana. All three became aspects of a triple moon-goddess (see *Il Penseroso*, l. 59 n.).

132. *Stygian*: See *L'Allegro*, l. 3 n.

176. *Pan*: See *Arcades*, ll. 106–7 n. and Nativity Ode, l. 89 n.

190. *Phoebus' wain*: the chariot of the sun-god.

230–7. Echo was a mountain nymph, in love with Narcissus, who would not return her love. She pined away, until nothing remained but her voice. As a punishment, Narcissus was made to fall in love with his own beauty, which he saw reflected in a pool; he hung over it, until he was transformed into a flower.

232. *Meander*: a river in Asia Minor, famous for its winding ('meandering') course.

252–61. The comparison of the Lady's singing to that of Circe and the Sirens serves to bring out the contrast between holy and unholy beauty, virtue and vicious pleasure. Comus, in referring to his mother Circe, surrounds himself with memories of enchantment. Milton has brought together elements from different sources, as he did in the previous reference to Circe (ll. 50–77); in the Odyssey the Sirens had nothing to do with Circe or her island, and were not directly connected with Scylla and Charybdis. But all these episodes from Homer had the same moral associations for Milton and other Renaissance poets; they represented temptation and danger, wandering and possible destruction.

Sirens three: singing maidens who by their music lured mariners to shipwreck on their rocks, as in the *Odyssey*, Book xii. See also l. 878.

Naiades: fresh-water nymphs, identified here with the four water-goddesses who wait on Circe in the *Odyssey*, Book x.

Elysium: Paradise in Greek religion. See l. 996 and *L'Allegro*, l. 148.

Scylla . . . Charybdis: a rock and a whirlpool opposite one another in the straits between Italy and Sicily. The rock was inhabited by a monster of the same name, which barked like a dog (*Odyssey*, Book xii). Odysseus successfully navigated the straits, in which a ship that tried to avoid one hazard was in danger from the other. In *The Faerie Queene*, Book II. xii. 3–9, Spenser uses a rock and a whirlpool as moral allegory, in the voyage of Guyon to the Bower of Bliss.

268. *Pan*: See l. 176 and *Arcades*, ll. 106–7 n.

Silvan: See *Il Penseroso*, l. 134 n.

267–70. Cf. the functions of the Genius of the Wood in *Arcades*, ll. 44–60.

290. *Hebe*: goddess of youth. See *L'Allegro*, l. 29.

334. *Chaos*: i.e. confusion. In Greek mythology Chaos was the disorderly heap of unshaped matter before creation, and was personified as the mother of Night (l. 335) and Erebus.

341–2. *star of Arcady Or Tyrian Cynosure*: Both these were pole stars, used for navigation by the Greeks and the Phoenicians respectively. The Phoenician or Tyrian pole star (which is also our own) was in the tail of the constellation of the Lesser Bear, which the Greeks called *Cynosura* (literally 'Dog's Tail'). The Greek pole star was Arcturus, i.e. the 'Watcher of the Bear' in the Greater Bear. It is 'of Arcady', because the Greeks said that the Greater Bear represented the mythical Arcadian princess Callisto; she was loved by Zeus, changed into a bear by the jealous Hera, and after her wanderings transformed into the constellation. Arcas, her son by Zeus, became Arcturus. 'Cynosure' came to mean any guiding star; see *L'Allegro*, l. 80.

393–6. Hesperus ('the evening star') presided over the Garden of the Hesperides, a paradise or island of the Blest in the Western Ocean. He was the father of the Hesperides, who helped a sleepless dragon to guard a tree bearing golden apples. See ll. 981–3.

422. The nymph with arrows is a follower of the goddess Diana, vowed to chastity. See ll. 441–6.

440–6. The moon-goddess Diana or Artemis was a huntress and patroness of virgins. The 'bolt of Cupid' is the arrow of the love-god. 'Hence' (l. 440) shows that Milton is giving an allegorical meaning to Diana's equipment (and Minerva's in the next lines); see Appendix I.

448–9. 'Minerva, virgin goddess of wisdom, was represented holding a shield with the Gorgon's head of Medusa in the centre;

the Gorgon's head, with its locks of serpents, turned the observer to stone' (Wright).

478. Apollo, the sun-god, was also the god of poetry, medicine, and philosophy; for the Greeks music was linked to all these. 'In the "Phaedo" Socrates is represented as the servant of Apollo, and in the "Republic" Plato remarks that philosophy tempered by music is the best friend and guardian of man's virtue' (Wright). For the lute, cf. *Love's Labour's Lost*, IV. iii:

> as sweet and musical
> As bright Apollo's lute, strung with his hair.

494. *Thyrsis*: a frequent name for shepherds in pastoral poetry. See *L'Allegro*, l. 83 n. The praise of Thyrsis as a musician is a second compliment to Henry Lawes (see ll. 86–8).

517. *Chimeras*: The Chimaera was a fabulous fire-breathing monster compounded of a lion, a dragon, and a goat; it became a term for any imaginary monster.

535. *Hecate*: Pronounce 'Hecat-e'. See ll. 129–36 n.

604. *Acheron*: Hades and its powers in general, as in classical poets; also the name of one of the four rivers of Hell.

605. *Harpies and Hydras*: malevolent monsters. Harpies were rapacious creatures with women's faces and the wings and claws of birds of prey; in Virgil (*Aeneid*, iii) they swoop down and defile or snatch away banquets. The Hydra was a snake-like beast with many heads, which grew again as fast as they were cut off.

619–28. The 'shepherd lad' here is Milton himself; the passage is a commemoration of his friendship with Henry Lawes. The singing of Thyrsis is the music of Lawes, which has been praised more than once already in the masque (see l. 494), and which Milton eulogizes later in Sonnet VIII. The shepherd lad's knowledge of herbs and plants is the young Milton's learning in moral and mystical philosophy, which was a preparation for his task as a poet. Milton represents himself modestly here ('of small regard to see to'), because he does not yet feel able to claim the status of a poet; even in *Lycidas*, written more than three years later, he is still 'the uncouth swain' (l. 186).

629–33. 'These lines describe the dark and difficult nature of philosophy, which can yet flower into poetry . . . . The statement that the plant does not flower in "this soil" refers to the Renaissance belief that the northern climates were not as congenial to poetic genius as those of Greece and Italy' (Wright).

636–7. In the *Odyssey*, Book x, moly is a white flower with a black root, which Hermes gives to Odysseus as a protection against the charms of Circe. Milton's first Latin elegy, written in 1626, uses the same symbolism: 'But I am preparing . . . to leave as soon as possible this city of delights [London] and, with the aid of the divine Moly, to flee far from the infamous halls of the faithless Circe.'

638. *Haemony*: an invented word, which may have been suggested by Haemonia, an old name for Thessaly, since Thessaly was famous for magic in ancient times. But it seems likely that Milton wished his mysterious root to have religious associations; and there may be a connection with the Greek word *haims*, 'blood', which would hint at the Redemption. The statement that haemony is *more* efficacious than moly (l. 636) is then a contrast between pagan wisdom and Christian faith. 'Guillaume Budé in *De Transitu Hellenismi ad Christianismum* had drawn a distinction between "moly Homericum" (representing Greek philosophical doctrine) and "moly nostrum" (the teaching of the Cross)' (Le Comte).

655. In Virgil (*Aeneid*, viii) one of the sons of Vulcan, Cacus, 'vomits a mass of smoke and wraps his dwelling in blind darkness'. Vulcan was the god of fire.

661–2. 'The nymph Daphne, fleeing from the amorous Apollo, was changed at her own entreaty into a laurel tree' (Wright).

675–6. Homer's Nepenthes brings mere indifference to grief, rather than positive well-being. In the *Odyssey*, Book iv, Helen (daughter of Jupiter by Leda) put the drug *Nepenthes* (cit. 'pain-dispelling') into her husband Menelaus' wine. 'A man felt no grief for the remainder of the day on which he drank it, "not though men slew his brother or dear son before his face"' (Elton). Polydamna, wife of Thone, King of Egypt, had given the drug to Helen, when she and Menelaus visited Egypt after the Trojan war.

707–8. The Cynics and Stoics despised all pleasures, and especially those of the senses.

Stoic fur: i.e. Stoic school of philosophy (referring to the academic gown faced with 'budge').

Cynic tub: The Cynic philosopher Diogenes showed his contempt for riches and social conventions by living in a tub, in the market-place of Athens.

803–5. 'Saturn's crew' were the Titans, sons of Heaven and Earth, whom Jove defeated with his thunderbolts, hurling them down to captivity in the underworld. Erebus was originally the black region on this side of Hades, but is used generally for Hell, as a place of darkness.

822. *Meliboeus*: The name of the first shepherd in Virgil's First Eclogue, who was traditionally identified with Virgil himself. Milton uses it to mean Spenser, the English poet for whom he had the highest esteem (l. 823), and who had told the story of Sabrina in *The Faerie Queene*, II. x. 17–19.

824–32. The original source of the story of Sabrina (or Sabra) is Geoffrey of Monmouth's *British History*; from there it passed into later chronicles and histories, including Milton's own unfinished *History of Britain*. Brute (l. 828) is Brutus, who was said by Geoffrey to be a descendant of Aeneas; he conquered Albion and renamed it Britain (after himself). His eldest son Locrine succeeded him as king, and married Gwendolen, who was the daughter of Corineus, the ruler of Cornwall. But Locrine fell in love with Estrildis, by whom he had a daughter, Sabra. Gwendolen raised an army in Cornwall, and defeated and killed Locrine. 'But not so ends the fury of Gwendolen: for Estrildis and her daughter Sabra she throws into a river: and, to leave a monument of revenge, proclaims that the stream be henceforth called after the daughter's name, which by length of time is now changed to Sabrina or Severn.' Spenser's version differs in its details from Geoffrey's, and Milton's from both (though he follows Geoffrey in the *History of Britain*).

833–51. Sabrina here becomes the Genius of the River; cf. Nativity Ode, ll. 181–8, the 'Genius of the Wood' in *Arcades* and *Il Penseroso*, l. 154, and *Lycidas*, ll. 183–5. The introduction of a local legend into the masque would have seemed appropriate and elegant to the audience; Sabrina had already appeared as the crowned goddess of the Severn in Drayton's *Polyolbion*, Song 6. But Milton is not merely being ingenious; his imagination was responsive to ancient British history and legend.

835. *Nereus*: the father of the Nereids, who lived at the bottom of

F

the sea. His age and kindliness are shown also in *The Faerie Queene*, III. iv, where he and his daughters tend a wounded mortal in their cave undersea. See l. 871.

838. *asphodel*: a flower which Homer describes as covering the fields at the entrance to the underworld, where Odysseus met the spirits of the dead. In poetry it became a symbol of immortal life. The name is given in Mediterranean countries to a not uncommon flower of the lily species.

859 89. The 'adjuring verse' is made up of a Song as opening invocation, and a call to the goddess to appear in the name of various water deities and their attributes.

868–82. *great Oceanus*: the god of primeval water and parent of all seas, rivers, springs, and lakes, both on earth and in the underworld. The early Greeks thought of the earth as a flat disc dividing Heaven from the lower world, or Tartarus. The Ocean was a stream flowing round the earth, which consisted only of Europe, Asia, and Africa (and in effect only of those parts of them which lay near enough to the Mediterranean to be explored).

869. *earth-shaking*: was the stock poetic epithet for the God of the Sea.

870. *Tethys*: wife of Oceanus, and in Homer the mother of all things, as Oceanus was the father; they lived in the far West, aloof and dignified.

871. *Nereus'*: See l. 835 n.

872. *Carpathian wizard's hook*: Proteus was a sea-god who could change his shape from one moment to another; he is called a wizard by Homer. His home was the Carpathian sea, i.e. the East Mediterranean (from the isle of Carpathus, between Crete and Rhodes). His 'hook' is a shepherd's crook with which he controlled the 'herds of Neptune', the seals.

873. Triton was a merman, the son of Neptune and Amphitrite, usually depicted blowing a shell-trumpet.

874. Glaucus was a fisherman of Boeotia, who by eating a certain herb became a sea-god with the gift of prophecy.

875–6. Leucothea (lit. 'white goddess') was the name taken by Ino, daughter of Cadmus, when she was turned into a sea-goddess;

her son was transformed with her, becoming Palaemon, god of harbours and beaches.

877. Thetis, a daughter of Nereus, who became the mother of Achilles, is called 'silver-footed' by Homer.

878. See ll. 252–61 n.

879–80. Parthenope was one of the Sirens; her tomb was supposed to be at Naples. Ligea is the name given to a sea-nymph by Virgil; Milton sees her as a mermaid (ll. 881–2), and so a type of Siren.

921. Amphitrite was the wife of Neptune, and so Queen of the Sea.

922–3. See ll. 824–32 n. Anchises was the father of Aeneas, who was the ancestor of the legendary Brutus who conquered Britain.

963–4. Mercury, the messenger of the Gods, was also the inventor of music and of gymnastic skill; the Dryades are wood nymphs, whom he delighted to lead in dancing. Since Mercury is above all a witty and sophisticated deity, he is an appropriate inventor of court dances.

976. *Ocean*: See ll. 868–82 n.

981–3. See ll. 393–5 n.

986. The Graces were three goddesses who gave joy and beauty to life. See *L'Allegro*, ll. 12 n. The Hours, personifying times and seasons, presided especially over the happier seasons of spring and summer, in association with the Graces and the Muses. See Sonnet I, l. 4.

992. *Iris*: goddess of the rainbow. See l. 83.

996. Cf. l. 257.

997. We are warned of an allegorical meaning in the lines that follow. Cf. *Il Penseroso*, l. 120.

999–1002. Adonis, a youth loved by Venus, delighted in hunting, and was killed by a wild boar which wounded him in the thigh (1000). By permission of the gods, he revived and spent half the year with Venus, and half in the underworld—but, according to Milton, sleeping in Elysium. Venus is called the 'Assyrian queen' to remind us of the Syrian origins of the myth (see Nativity Ode, l. 204 n.). She sits 'on the ground' because she represents earthly

love; Cupid is 'far above' in the air because he stands here for
heavenly love (but cf. l. 445).

1003–11. Venus and Adonis represent earthly love and its object,
physical beauty which grows, fades, and dies; Cupid and Psyche
represent heavenly love and its object the soul, which may suffer,
but endures, and cannot die. In the legend of the loves of Cupid and
Psyche (told by Apuleius in *The Golden Ass*), Psyche (lit. 'the soul')
is separated from her lover Cupid by the jealousy of his mother
Venus. She has to undergo many trials and sufferings, but her love
surmounts them all, and at length the gods decree that the lovers
shall be reunited in heaven.

Lycidas

(November 1637)

When Milton heard of Edward King's death, in the autumn of
1637, he had been thinking of his future as a poet, but he had written
no English verse for about three years (though he had revised *Comus*
for its anonymous publication in 1637). He was now asked to
contribute to a volume of memorial verse, to be published at
Cambridge by King's friends. Edward King was younger than
Milton, but they had been at Christ's College together. King had
become a fellow of the College and was intending to enter the
Church. The memorial volume published by his friends early in
1638 contained twenty-three poems in Latin and Greek and thirteen
in English, and indicates that he had been very generally admired
and loved. While we do not know him as one of Milton's closest
friends, *Lycidas* is the best evidence that his death came as a personal
loss.

In the verse of *Lycidas* Milton is re-creating the music of Virgil's
Eclogues, in which the Latin hexameter is used for both dialogue
and song. He wants to give the effect of spontaneous, intense emotion
rising and falling, as he looks back on past happiness and tries to
accept the fact of death. For this purpose he turned again to the
Italian *canzone* tradition (see the Nativity Ode and *On Time*, n.), but
applied the principles he found there to construct a large-scale lyric
such as had never been achieved in English. He limits his lines to the
two types normal in Italian; in English they are of ten syllables

(five stresses) and six syllables (three stresses), the latter being used sparingly. The poem is in verse-paragraphs of varying length, in which the rhymes are interwoven in varying patterns. In a *canzone* the different parts of a stanza were linked by a *chiave* or 'key' rhyme; Milton uses such 'keys'—a line rhyming with at least two preceding rhymes, but leading to a new series (e.g. ll. 6, 108, 136, 170). The paragraphs always close on a rhyme, and often on a rhymed couplet. There are unrhymed lines scattered throughout (e.g. ll. 1, 13, 15, 22, 39, 51, 82), but strong and close rhyme predominates, so that the unrhymed lines are hardly apparent, and yet allow the poet greater freedom. The concluding eight-line stanza is suggested by the *commiato* or envoy of a *canzone*: it is a farewell to the poem (as the poem is a farewell to youth), contrasting in its calm with the storm of grief that has now blown over.

Milton writes in *Lycidas* as a shepherd mourning a dead companion; the poem is a pastoral, a form whose conventions went back, through Renaissance imitations, to the Greek and Roman classical poetry. Pastoral poetry as a literary form began in the third century B.C., with the eclogues of the Greek poet Theocritus. He wrote of the life of Sicilian shepherds, and was followed in Greek by Bion and Moschus, and in Latin by Virgil (70–19 B.C.). The shepherd's life is in obvious contrast to that of the warrior, the other archetypal figure in primitive societies; he leads a peaceful life close to nature, with much leisure for song or other amusements. Not much skill or strength is needed to look after sheep; it can be done by the young, or even children. Pastoral poetry therefore becomes a picture of carefree youth, love and friendship and song; and in its sophisticated Renaissance revival it turns into a picture of young poets or scholars, before they enter on the cares and dangers of adult life. Consequently it often becomes an autobiography in disguise, a way of writing about oneself and one's fellow poets.

A late but very important development of the pastoral conventions was to make the shepherds represent, not only poets and scholars, but priests. This grew naturally out of the Gospel metaphor of 'the good shepherd' for Christ, from his charge to St. Peter, 'Feed my sheep', and from the conception of bishops and clergy as 'shepherds of a flock'. Thus pastoral verse came to satirize bad priests and corruption in the Church, and in this *Lycidas* follows Petrarch and the Latin poets of the Renaissance, and Spenser in *The Shepheardes Calender*.

Within the pastoral tradition the pastoral elegy had become a distinct form. Most classical eclogues showed shepherds competing in singing-matches or praising their lovers; but the lament for a dead shepherd produces some of the most beautiful, such as Virgil's elegy for a fellow poet, his friend Gallus.

There are eleven verse-paragraphs in *Lycidas*, each expressing a movement of the thought or feeling (and some a conflict within themselves, as in ll. 64–84 and 132–64). But the poem can be divided into four main sections, followed by the envoy:

(i) ll. 1–49. The young poet declares that he is forced by the death of his fellow poet to pay tribute in verse, though his art is not yet mature (1–14). He will compel the Muses to sing (as he hopes some poet may sing at his own death), since he and Lycidas were friends from childhood (15–24). He looks back to their work and pastimes together (25–36), and feels that the countryside mourns for the death of the shepherd (37–49).

(ii) ll. 50–84. But if nature sympathizes, why did not the nature-spirits (the nymphs) save the poet they loved from death? But they could have done nothing, since even Orpheus, the most famous of all poets, was not rescued from death by his mother, who was a Muse (50–63). If the Muses themselves are ungrateful and will not protect their servants, why should poets strive to master their art—would it not be better to seek pleasure? Desire of fame persuades them to effort and self-sacrifice, yet all their hopes can be suddenly frustrated by death. But a voice from Heaven answers that true fame is granted by God, not by men, and virtue will never go unrewarded (64–84).

(iii) ll. 85–131. The poet returns to the pastoral theme, after the flash of prophetic vision (85–8), and questions the elements as to the manner of his friend's death (89–102). After nature and the poets, learning and religion mourn for the dead youth. The river-god of the Cam, representing Cambridge, and St. Peter, representing the universal Church, appear in procession; and Peter wishes that Lycidas could have lived, rather than the bad shepherds who flourish at the expense of their flock (113–29). But the wrath of God will fall on them (130–1).

(iv) ll. 132–85. Again the pastoral Muses must be summoned back, after the denunciation of evil and the prophecy of doom (132–3). The poet and his friends must cast flowers in heaps on the bier of the dead shepherd (the flowers are emblems of poetry as well as of beauty and youth). But the scattering of flowers cannot disguise the fact that the body is lost at sea (152–3); whether it has been carried to the north, or south towards Spain, may the powers of Heaven and the sea take pity on it (154–64). But the shepherds must now cease mourning, for Lycidas is not dead: he has sunk beneath the sea only to rise again like the sun, through the power of Christ, and he now shares Heaven's glory with the saints (165–81). He is rewarded also by being made protector of those who travel on the sea where he was drowned (183–5).—The last stanza stands back from the poem, and turns away to the future.

If we thus divide the poem, we see that the first section leads to the central theme, the poet's death, by way of Milton's own dedication to poetry and his youthful studies shared with King. The waste and pathos of early death are considered in each of the three sections that follow, and each rises to a religious climax (ll. 83–4; 130–1; and 172–85). The two so-called 'digressions' (on fame and the Church) —which Milton himself admits transgress the limits of pastoral— are really stages on the way to the final affirmation of faith.

The untimely death of a young man or woman, one of our contemporaries, can be a momentous experience, bringing us a sense of the reality of death, and that an epoch of our own life has ended. Milton responds intensely to this not uncommon experience; *Lycidas* dramatizes sorrow, the sense of loss, but also the renewed vision of life that is born of it—of the human lot, and the poet's life as a part of it. There is nothing here to cast doubt on the depth of Milton's friendship or feeling for Edward King. He does what the living have always done for the dead they have known and loved. The ritual mourning of all religions is meant to purge emotion and bring appeasement of sorrow. *Lycidas* is impassioned ritual; its following of poetic forms and precedents is a way to organize and universalize grief.

We know that the closest friend of Milton's youth was Charles Diodati; but Edward King recalled Cambridge, and young men discovering companionship in their interests and hopes. For this it would be hard to find a better emblem than Milton's compressed pastoral scene (25–36); the two young herdsmen following the cycle of work and rest, in a fresh and friendly countryside of hills and valleys. The repetitiveness of country life—the cool twilight of dawn, the peaceful drowsiness of noonday, the dewy evening—is seen in retrospect, from a distance, as a lost paradise. Throughout the poem such delicious pastoral beauty is contrasted with the sterner, vaster beauty of mountain- and sea-scapes which frame the death of Lycidas (50–5, 59–63, 91–5). By such changes of setting and perspective Milton dramatizes the frailty of human life and happiness; the culmination is the contrast between the flower-passage and the huge Atlantic seas that wash the lost body, tiny in comparison, to and fro.

In *Lycidas* Milton uses the pastoral convention, but in a characteristically bold and original way: the poem is a tumultuous but ordered meditation on human life, and on his own task as interpreter of its meaning. His personal involvement charges every detail with double and triple meanings: the shepherd is both poet and priest, he is loved by God, and perhaps therefore must suffer and die young. The water that drowns the poet, whether Lycidas or Orpheus, is a form of death that opens the way to eternal life. The 'day-star' that sets and rises again is both Apollo and Christ, and the poet who is servant to both. 'The still Morn' that fades and passes while the shepherd-mourner sings is Milton's youth; when he has finished his song, he turns away from the past and looks forward to new poetic tasks, 'fresh woods and pastures new'. The example of Virgil authorized Renaissance poets to exercise their art in pastoral as a preparation for writing an epic (Tasso and Spenser had exploited this convention). Milton uses the pastoral form both to present his youth as a poet and to imply that his vocation and life-work will be the epic.

1–3. Laurel, myrtle, and ivy have symbolic meanings. Woven together, they made a crown for the poet, the laurel being sacred to Apollo, the myrtle to Venus, the ivy to Bacchus. Milton means that he is returning to poetry, to make a garland for a fellow poet. The berries are unripe, the leaves have not yet been brought fully out by the season, because Milton is still perfecting his art.

8. Lycidas is the name of a shepherd in Virgil's ninth Eclogue, and also in the Seventh Idyl of Theocritus.

14. *melodious tear*: The Latin *lacrimae* was used to mean an elegy, and the metaphor had passed into English.

15–16. *Sisters of the sacred well*: The nine Muses, goddesses of

learning and the arts, had their holy place by a spring which rose at
the foot of Mount Olympus (from where Jove and the other
'Olympians' ruled the universe).

23–36. The description of the two young shepherds at work and
play is an allegory of life at Cambridge. The old shepherd Damoetas
who enjoys their 'song' represents an approving tutor. The cycle of
country life, unchanging in change and fostered by nature, is
represented by the shepherds' day. 'The star that rose' is the morning
star, which by evening has moved across to the west; Hesper
(evening star) is the same as Phosphor (morning star). Noonday is
evoked by the 'sultry' hum of the gray-fly.

9. Cf. *Measure for Measure*, IV. ii. 'Looke, th' unfolding Starre
calles up the Shepheard, and *Comus*, l. 93: 'The star that bids the
shepherd fold'.

34. *Satyrs . . . Fauns*: In Greek and Roman religion these were
half-human, half-animal beings associated with untamed nature and
country life. Fauns were supposed to have feet like goats, satyrs were
shaggy and had tails.

46. *taint-worm*: a disease in cattle.

48. *white-thorn*: hawthorn.

50–5. Virgil (*Eclogues* x. 9–12), echoing Theocritus, *Idylls* i.
66–9, had made his shepherd-mourner ask the nymphs where they
were when Gallus was dying. Mona is Anglesey, Deva is the river
Dee; the Druids were said to be buried in the mountains of Denbigh-
shire (ll. 52–3). King embarked from Chester, on the Dee; the
places mentioned are near the Irish Sea, where he was drowned.

53. *bards*: 'an ancient Celtic order of minstrels who preserved in
their verse the traditions, laws, and religious precepts of their nation'
(Wright). Similar functions were attributed by Roman writers to
the Druids, who were priests.

55. Spenser, Drayton, and other Elizabethan poets associated the
Dee with magic ('wizard stream'). The river was formerly the
boundary between England and Wales, and was surrounded by
many legends and superstitions. Milton was deeply interested in
ancient British history and culture; cf. *Comus*, l. 33, etc.

56–7. 'Alas, it is foolish of me to imagine what might have

happened "if you had been there"—for what difference could that have made?'

58. In Greek mythology Orpheus is the archetype of a poet, whose songs could persuade even death to relent (see *L'Allegro*, ll. 145–50 n.). He was the son of Calliope, the muse of epic poetry, and died by being torn to pieces by the Maenads, followers of Bacchus; they threw his head into the river Hebrus, in Thrace; it floated down to the sea and was carried across to the isle of Lesbos. The legend of Orpheus, who was both poet and musician, seems to have had a personal meaning for Milton, who refers to his death again in *P.L.* vii. 32–38. Here Orpheus is, like Lycidas, a poet destroyed by senseless forces; the story is made to convey helpless love and grief.

59. 'Enchanting' has its literal meaning of charming by means of song: Orpheus tamed wild beasts and moved rocks and trees by his singing.

65. *shepherd's trade*: i.e. the profession of poetry; but the shepherd is a symbol for the scholar and priest as well as the poet, as we see later in the poem (ll. 103–31). The 'trade' of shepherd is 'homely' and 'slighted' because learning and the Church were generally regarded as somewhat inferior professions.

68–9. Amaryllis and Neaera are frequent names in pastorals, for maidens loved by the shepherds.

71. Milton refers also later, in *P.R.* ii. 227–8 and iii. 25–8, to the desire of fame as likely to be the one source of weakness in men of fine character.

75. *the blind Fury*: Atropos, one of the three Fates, who cut the thread of life; the others were Clotho, who spun the thread, and Lachesis, who measured it out. By calling her a Fury, and blind, Milton emphasizes death as a senseless, destructive force.

76. *But not the praise*: death cuts off life, but not the reward of a life lived well.

77. Phoebus replies to Milton's doubts because he is god of poetry, but also of prophecy, and can therefore be a mouthpiece of Jove, the supreme God. In Virgil's Eclogue vi Phoebus admonishes the poet by taking him by the ear; Milton's ears 'tremble' with a sudden thrill of fear.

81–4. 'As ruler of gods and men Jupiter sees and judges all things, watches over truth and justice, and is invoked as witness to all oaths' (Wright).

85–6. Arethusa (see *Arcades*, ll. 29–31 n.) and Mincius represent the pastoral poetry of Greece and Rome. Theocritus refers in his first Idyll to the spring of Arethusa, in Sicily; Virgil, who was born near the River Mincius, at Mantua in Northern Italy, describes it in his seventh Eclogue. See ll. 132–3.

89. *The Herald of the Sea*: Triton, usually depicted with a horn made of a sea-shell. See *Comus*, l. 873.

90. Neptune was the god of the sea.

96. *Hippotades*: 'Son of Hippotas', i.e. Aeolus; he was supposed to keep the winds imprisoned in a cavern on his island (see l. 97).

99. Panope and her sisters are Nereids, i.e. sea-nymphs, who were well disposed towards sailors. See *Comus*, l. 835.

100–2. The ship was wrecked, not by a storm, but by striking a rock. It was 'ill-fated', built and equipped in unlucky circumstances. Eclipses were believed to portend disaster.

102. *sacred head*: beloved head.

103–31. Camus, the river Cam, representing the University of Cambridge, and St. Peter, representing the Church, come at the end of what is thought of as a procession of gods and spirits, mourning the dead shepherd: cf. Shelley's procession of mourners for the dead Keats in *Adonais*.

104. The 'hairy' mantle, and the bonnet or cap made of sedge, are appropriate dress for the river-god, representing the woods and reeds along the water's edge.

105. *figures dim*: half legible or cryptic marks. Perhaps they signify the uncertain origins of the University, lost in the past.

106. 'That sanguine flower' is the hyacinth, which was supposed to have sprung from the blood of Hyacinthus; he was loved by the god Apollo, who killed him accidentally by throwing a quoit. Apollo changed the boy's blood into the flower and recorded his grief on the petals, which were said to have written on them, in Greek, *AI, AI* (alas!).

109. St. Peter was a fisherman of the Sea of Galilee. See Luke 5: 1–11. Christ gave Peter the keys which opened the way to

salvation; see Matthew 16: 19. The Church developed the notion of two keys, one to open for the blessed and one to shut out the damned.

111. He wears a mitre as the first bishop of the Church, 'the prince of the Apostles'.

112-32. St. Peter denounces the corrupt element among the Anglican clergy, those who took holy orders only to obtain a living, not because they had any vocation for the priesthood. Edward King, like many other Cambridge men, intended to, or was about to, be ordained as a clergyman; Milton himself, when he first went to Cambridge, must have had that possibility in mind for himself. But he decided against it, partly because of the conditions in the Church which he here attacks. The distinction between the true and the false shepherd, i.e. priest or religious leader, goes back to the New Testament.

115. 'He that entereth not by the door into the sheepfold, but climbeth up by some other way, the same is a thief and a robber' (John 10). Compare *P.L.* iv. 193:

> So clomb this first grand thief [i.e. Satan] into God's fold,
> So since into his church lewd hirelings climb.

117. The pastoral convention is brilliantly exploited in the satire on the wicked clergy. Notice the succession of strong, harsh, words from common speech: *bellies, creep, scramble, shove, mouths; recks, grate, rank, rot*, etc.

117. i.e. snatch the emoluments of the Church. Sheep-shearing, like the seasons when various crops were gathered, was celebrated by a festival.

119. *Blind mouths*: the mixed metaphor (which becomes more mixed when the 'mouths' are said to be unable to hold sheep-hooks, or learn the shepherd's art) conveys passionate scorn. A creature interested only in feeding itself, i.e. looking after its own physical well-being, is the antithesis of a good priest, who looks to the interests of others.

123-7. The shepherds' songs are a metaphor for sermons. The bad clergy preach seldom and poorly, providing little instruction or edification. The seventeenth-century Puritans thought preaching all-important; the Anglicans produced many great preachers, but (apart from differences of doctrine) they were criticized by the Puritans for not making the sermon central or even essential to their services.

125. The congregation expect some spiritual nourishment when they 'look up' to the priest in his pulpit; but they get nothing but words ('wind') or false doctrine ('rank mist').

128–9. The 'grim wolf' is the Church of Rome, which was thought to be making converts because of the inadequacy of the Church of England. The Anglican bishops were popularly, though unjustly, suspected of being favourable to the Roman Church ('and nothing said').

130–1. The threat of retribution in these lines is the more effective for the mysteriousness with which it is expressed. The 'two-handed engine' must be either an axe or a sword, both double-edged. Christ had used the metaphor of an axe for the coming judgement of God (Matthew 3: 10 and Luke 3: 9): 'and now the ax is laid to the root of the tree: therefore every tree which bringeth not forth good fruit is hewn down.' Milton in 1641 wrote of the Bishops 'feeling the ax of God's reformation hewing at the old and hollow trunk of Popery'. But the image of an axe goes together with that of a tree to be cut down. Here it is better to take the double-edged weapon as the sword of God's justice. 'The door' remains mysterious, but suggests the Last Judgement, as the way to Heaven or Hell.

132–51. Milton reinvokes the Muse of Pastoral, and asks for all the flowers of the countryside to be strown on his friend's body. Offerings of flowers are frequent in pastoral poetry. Garlands are thrown on the body in Bion's lament for Adonis; flowers are called upon to mourn in Moschus' Lament for Bion. But Milton may owe more to Shakespeare's flower-passages—Perdita's list in *The Winter's Tale* or those scattered for Fidele in *Cymbeline*.

132. The river Alpheus was in love with the nymph Arethusa, and is thus associated with Sicilian pastoral. See l. 85 n. and *Arcades*, 29–31 n. 'The dread voice' is that of religion. Renaissance poets regarded religious poetry as the highest form of art; when it spoke, other voices should be silent.

138. 'The swart star' is the dog-star, or Sirius, commonly used in classical poetry to indicate summer heat, as it is prominent in the sky

in August. Here it is called 'swarthy' because it darkens or scorches vegetation. The 'lap' is that of the valley of l. 136.

142. Milton is remembering the lines in *The Winter's Tale*, IV. iii. 122–4, in which the primrose dies before it can see the summer sun:

> pale primroses
> That die unmarried, ere they can behold
> Bright Phoebus in his strength.

146. Both the honeysuckle and the bindweed (wild convolvulus) were called woodbines.

149. *Amaranthus*: a generic name for love-lies-bleeding.

154–62. Lost in the Irish Sea, the body could have been washed either north, to the west coast of Scotland, or south, to Cornwall and the Bay of Biscay.

159. 'Moist vows' can mean prayers accompanied by tears; and would then refer to the poem itself (called a 'tear' in l. 14), which is 'denied' the body of the dead man; or it could mean the prayers which his friends had put up for his safety, and would then refer to the custom in antiquity of making votive offerings to Neptune, either to be granted safety at sea, or to give thanks for having escaped danger. The sense would then be that Lycidas was not preserved by such prayers ('denied' to our 'vows').

160. Land's End in Cornwall was called the promontory of Bellerium by the Romans; it was 'so named from Bellerus a Cornish giant', according to Warton. But Milton may have invented Bellerus, for he does not occur in ancient British legends.

161. *the guarded Mount*: St. Michael's Mount in Cornwall, near Land's End; it is a large rock connected by a causeway with the shore at low water, an island at high tide. Like Mont St. Michel in Brittany, it was the site of a monastery in the Middle Ages, and remained a fortress later. There was a legend that the Archangel Michael had appeared to some hermits on the crags of the rock; this is the 'vision' Milton refers to. He imagines that St. Michael still presides over the rock and protects England from the enmity of Spain. It is likely that the medieval monastery was crowned by a statue of the Archangel, and that Milton had this in mind.

162. *Namancos*: near Cape Finisterre; like the Castle of Bayona, it is on the north coast of Spain, looking towards England. Milton

has all the associations of the Armada in mind when he imagines the Cornish coast as guarded by St. Michael.

163. St. Michael is asked to look 'homeward', i.e. to relax his watch on the Atlantic and Spain, in order to look for Lycidas.

164. The dolphins, friendly sea-creatures, are asked to float the body ashore. There is an allusion to the Greek story of another poet, Arion. He threw himself into the sea to escape from a ship, the crew of which were threatening him, and was brought to shore on the back of a dolphin which had been delighted by his songs.

181. See Isaiah 25: 8 and Rev. 7: 17.

165–85. The change from lament to triumph is a feature of the Christianized pastoral elegy of the Renaissance; it is foreshadowed by Virgil's picture of 'Daphnis at Heaven's Gate' in Eclogue v. In Spenser's elegy for Dido in the November Eclogue of *The Shepheardes Calender*, the refrain 'O heavie herse . . . O carefull verse' is changed towards the end to 'O happye herse . . . O joyfull verse'. In his *Daphnaida* the refrain 'Weepe Shepheard weepe to make my undersong' becomes 'Cease Shepheard, cease, and end thy undersong'.

183. *the Genius of the shore*: In Greek and Roman religion the *genius loci* inhabited and protected a particular place, and was often worshipped at a small local shrine. See Nativity Ode, ll. 181–8 n. Since in Roman religion the dead could be honoured as gods, they could also become *genii loci*. Virgil makes the shepherds adopt their dead friend Daphnis as a local god and protector.

186–93. The switch to the third person ('the uncouth swain') gives the sense of the mourner detaching himself from his sorrow, which has been relieved by the very process of expressing it, and so 'understanding' it.

189. *Doric lay*: Theocritus and Moschus wrote their Sicilian pastorals in the Doric dialect, because Syracuse in Sicily was a Dorian colony.

The Sonnets

(1629, 1632, 1642–1658)

The sonnet was introduced into England from Italy in the sixteenth century by Sir Thomas Wyatt (1503–42), and in various modified forms yielded some of the finest Elizabethan poetry. But the English passion for sonneteering died out in the early seventeenth century, and it is almost irrelevant to Milton's sonnet-writing, which represents a fresh start. His was an individual undertaking, and unique in the mid seventeenth century; but it was also more closely related to the Italian tradition, and more disciplined in style, than any earlier sonnet-writing in English.

Petrarch (1304–74) had established the sonnet as the perfect instrument for serious love-poetry (though it had been used, and was still to be used, for many other purposes). The Italian form is made up of fourteen lines, divided into eight (the octave) and six (the sestet). Octave and sestet each has its own set of rhymes, which hold it together; but each is also subdivided, the octave into two quatrains, the sestet into two tercets. In the octave the usual arrangement of rhymes was *abba abba* (though *abab abab* and *abab baba* also occurred). In the sestet two or three rhyme sounds were allowed, and their arrangement varied more widely than in the octave. In Italian sonnets it was normal for the sentences to fit into the divisions of the stanza, so that there would be pauses at the end of each quatrain and tercet, and a more marked pause between octave and sestet.

But Milton, while accepting Petrarch as the master of the form, adopted the stylistic innovations made by Petrarch's Renaissance followers, Bembo (1470–1547), Della Casa (1503–56), and Tasso (1544–95). These innovations aimed at bringing the sonnet closer to Latin classical verse, and particularly to the stately diction of Virgil and Horace. So the sentence structure became more complex, and the rhythm was slowed down; the syntax tended to overflow the two main and the two subsidiary divisions of the poem (though the effect still depended on these being felt, below the surface). The new style was to be exploited in epic verse by Tasso, and Milton's use of it in the Sonnets foreshadows the methods of his later blank verse, where we also find 'the sense variously drawn out from one verse into another'.

Milton's Sonnets are occasional poems (in the sense of poems arising out of a particular set of circumstances) in the grand epic manner. The technical changes he takes over from the Renaissance Italians make what is necessarily a short poem into one that seems weighty and sustained: pauses *within* the lines are added to those suggested by the rhymes, which may be partly submerged by the flow of the sense, but remain in our consciousness, since they are generally full-sounding and sometimes obtrusive (as in VI and VII). The sonnet becomes a single verse-paragraph flowing through a sound-pattern made up of the four divisions marked by the rhymes (see V, XII, XIII, XV).

One of Milton's favourite devices is an opening which addresses the recipient of the Sonnet, sometimes by name, and attaches descriptive phrases and relative clauses which may take up the first four lines (IV, VIII, XI, XVII), the first eight lines (V), or more (XII, XIII). A slow-moving opening in this or some other form (XV has a relative clause of time) will be followed by a central more direct statement, which will act as a pivot, leading to further points or reflections; these are sometimes leisurely (III, 10–14, V, 12–14, VIII, 12–14, XVI, 13–14, XVII, 11–14) and sometimes more urgent (XII, XIV, XV). The closing lines of Milton's Sonnets aim at an effect of fullness and finality. This may be reached by means of a religious idea (II, IV, IX, XIII, XIV, XV, XVII, XVIII), or a moral maxim (VII, X, XI, XVI, XVII, XVIII)—these cannot always be distinguished from each other.

A general characteristic of the Sonnets is their tendency to move out into a wider view or range of reference. London's danger spreads out over land and sea, and into the past, to Thebes and Athens (III); a serious English girl is led gently into the glimmering midnight hour of a Gospel parable (IV); a court composer is reminded of the shades of Dante's Purgatory (VIII); and the poet in his blindness is absorbed into a vision of God's power embracing Heaven and earth (XV).

Many of Milton's Sonnets belong to the category of Tasso's Heroic Sonnets, in which he addressed great men of his time. The idea of heroic greatness in both poets demanded the religious view of life, and no clear line can be drawn between Milton's poems addressed to public men or inspired by international events (XIV), those written for friends (IV, V, XVI, XVII), and his more intimate religious meditations (II, XV); all these types come together in XVIII.

I. The order in which Milton printed the Sonnets has been generally accepted as chronological, and the dates which can be established for the composition of some of them support that assumption. Hence the sonnet to the nightingale is probably the

earliest, written about 1629 when he was twenty. Two of the Latin
Elegies, V and VII, belonging to that period, celebrate the coming
of spring and the power of love over the adolescent's imagination.

Milton writes as a lover and a poet. It is spring, and he begs the
nightingale to sing before the cuckoo, because this is for a lover an
omen of good luck. Here he is using a medieval superstition, which
he found in a poem called 'The Cuckoo and the Nightingale', then
attributed to Chaucer: the writer, Sir Thomas Clanvowe, complains
that he has heard the cuckoo before the nightingale at the beginning
of May (the season of love), and that he is therefore doomed to
disappointment in love; but he hopes to have better luck next year.
Milton adds that the nightingale has had no reason not to favour
him, for he is a follower of both love and song, and the nightingale
must be the companion of one or the other, if not both.

The sonnet has an undertone of diffidence and humour (apparent
in the exaggeration of 'rude bird of hate' and 'hopeless doom').
While the imagery and diction are rather conventional, the music
of the language and the sustained flow of the sentences are strikingly
beautiful; and the last two lines make a memorable close.

9. *bird of hate*: In folklore and medieval poetry the cuckoo has a
bad reputation, as foisting its young on other birds; it signifies
deception in marriage and discord in love.

II. Modern scholars date this sonnet 9 December 1632, which was
Milton's 24th birthday; their conclusion is based on his habit of
writing (whether in English or Latin) 'in the 17th year of [his] age';
when we would write 'at the age of 17', i.e. 'in the 18th year'. Thus
the poem was written in the winter after Milton left Cambridge,
and when he had already decided to spend some years more in study.
There is a version in the Trinity MS., where it is attached to two
drafts of a letter to an unnamed friend, who had advised Milton to
choose a profession, and preferably the Church, rather than pursue
his studies. (It is significant that 23 is, according to Canon Law, the
age at which a man becomes eligible for Holy Orders.) Like many
of Milton's poems, this begins with misgivings, but ends with an
affirmation of faith.

1–4. 'Time is swiftly carrying me on through my youth, and as
yet I have achieved nothing.'

bud or blossom: The imagery suggests that Milton has in mind poetic achievement (as one might expect). In Latin *flos*, 'flower', was used as a metaphor for poetry.

5–8. 'I am younger in appearance than in fact, and I give even less evidence of mental maturity, such as other young men have been able to show.'

some more timely-happy spirits: may be suggested by such young poets of the day as Thomas Randolph and Abraham Cowley; the latter was only 14 in 1632, but about to publish his *Poetical Blossoms* (see l. 4, 'blossom'). The book is dated 1633, but Milton may have seen an early copy or heard of its existence. However, we are not obliged to look for a specific reference. For the absence of 'ripeness' see also *Lycidas*, ll. 3–5.

9–12. 'Yet whether I attain more or less maturity of mind, whether it comes soon or late, it will always be wholly submitted to the lot in life which God leads me to, whatever that should be.'

13–14. Some modern scholars have put forward an alternative reading: 'All that matters is whether I have grace to use my abilities in accordance with the will of God, as one ever in his sight.'

III. The MS. version of the sonnet has the title *When the assault was intended to the city* [of London], replacing a deleted title *On his door when the city expected an assault*; the date *1642* was inserted in the margin, and later deleted. We need not imagine that Milton ever pinned the sonnet to the door of his house in Aldersgate Street, or meant to do so.

The poem is usually dated November 1642 (though May 1641 has been proposed). At the beginning of the Civil War in August 1642, it was expected that the Royalist forces, based on Oxford, would attempt to take London; and after the Battle of Edgehill on 23 October, when the military advantage remained with the King, his army marched towards the capital, the Royalist cavalry under Prince Rupert plundering the country as they went. There was much alarm in London, and the Parliament made rapid preparations to defend it. On 12 November the Royalists met and defeated a Parliamentary force at Brentford, which was taken and sacked. But the next day the threat to the city was averted, when the King's army found itself faced with 24,000 men drawn up in order of battle at Turnham Green, decided it was outnumbered, and withdrew.

Smart has said: 'It may be believed that the sonnet was actually composed during the period of alarm, and before the retreat from Turnham Green on 13 November. While suspense and anxiety prevailed around him in the city, Milton, with his inflexible composure, remained calm and detached, and converted the moment of peril into a theme for slightly playful verse.' It is the apparent calm of the poem which has led Honigmann to suggest an earlier date, May 1641, when Londoners were also alarmed by a Royalist plot to seize the city; the threat was then less imminent, it was not preceded by Royalist successes and rumours of pillage, and Milton had not yet published any pamphlets against the King's party, and could reasonably claim to be given the immunity he asks for, as a poet's privilege. Honigmann's dating requires us to believe that the MS. date *1642* was a mistake, and deleted as such: this seems unlikely. Moreover, Milton presented poetry as his main vocation, even in the midst of bitter ecclesiastical controversy, early in 1642, in *The Reason of Church Government*; and he habitually showed courage in the face of danger.

The movement of the sonnet widens out from the grim possibilities of defeat in war—the armed men, the helpless private house—to remote lands and times, and echoes of the magnanimity of conquerors. The poet's quiet suburban house becomes the bower of the Muses, the walls of London are seen as the walls of ancient Athens; though they were saved 'from ruin bare' in the past, they represent greatness ruined by time. Yet the two far-off historic incidents also evoke what cannot be destroyed by time—poetry.

2. *defenceless doors*: Milton's house, being just outside the city-wall, could be said to be undefended.

9. *Muses' bower*: Milton lived in 'a pretty Garden-House' (Phillips), and always thought of himself as dwelling with the Muses.

10–12. *Emathian conqueror*: Alexander the Great, who sacked Thebes in 333 B.C. Emathia was a province of Macedonia, and the original seat of the Macedonian monarchy. Pliny is the source of the story about Alexander's sparing the poet Pindar's house, when he destroyed the rest of Thebes.

12–14. When the Spartan general Lysander and his allies captured Athens in 404 B.C., it was proposed in a council of war to raze the city. 'Yet afterwards, when there was a meeting of the captains together, a man of Phocis singing the first chorus of Euripides' *Electra* . . . they were all melted with compassion, and it seemed to be a cruel deed to destroy and pull down a city which had been so famous and produced such men' (Plutarch, *Life of Lysander*).

IV. The sonnet may be dated between 1642 and 1645 (when it was printed). The identity of the girl to whom it was addressed is not known. The circumstances are indicated in ll. 6–7: the girl was devout, and had been criticized as pretentious and priggish by people who did not like her; Milton comforts her, complimenting her on the beauty of her character and surrounding it with a Biblical solemnity and tenderness.

The language of parable and allegory is bare, and it would be merely confusing to make the images ('way', 'hill', 'lamp') richer. Nevertheless there is the bright touch of 'green' at the beginning, and in the last six lines the lamp seems to burn clearly in shadows, and finally in a mysterious midnight hour. Cf. *Il Penseroso*, l. 85.

2–4. 'The contrast between the easy way of vice and the toilsome upward path of virtue is familiar in ancient literature' (Smart). 'The broad way' comes directly from Christ's words: '. . . wide is the gate, and broad is the way, that leadeth to destruction' (Matt. 7: 13); it is green because of its pleasantness (cf. 'the primrose path of dalliance' in *Hamlet*, I. iii). Truth is also reached by climbing a hill in Donne's Third Satire.

5. Mary in the New Testament and Ruth in the Old Testament became types of Christian womanhood, in theology and art. Ruth the Moabitess chose to go with her mother-in-law Naomi when she returned to the land of Israel: 'thy people shall be my people, and thy God my God' (Ruth 1: 16). Mary, the sister of Martha, sat at Jesus' feet, 'and heard his word'; she became an emblem of the life of prayer, Christ having said, 'Mary hath chosen that good part, which shall not be taken away from her' (Luke 10: 39, 42).

7. *fret*: Suggested by the behaviour of Martha, who 'was cumbered about much serving, and came to him, and said, Lord, dost thou not care that my sister hath left me to serve alone?' (Honigmann).

8. *ruth*: Rhyme between words of the same sound but different meaning were not uncommon in medieval and Renaissance verse.

10–14. The final Biblical allusion, from which Milton extracts most beauty, is to the parable of the Ten Virgins, 'which took their lamps, and went forth to meet the bridegroom'. The wise virgins took oil for their lamps (l. 10), the foolish did not. 'And at midnight there was a cry made, Behold, the bridegroom cometh; go ye out to meet him. Then all those virgins arose, and trimmed their lamps.' But those without oil had to buy it. 'And while they went to buy, the bridegroom came; and they that were ready went in with him to the marriage: and the door was shut.' The bridegroom represents 'the Son of Man', the readiness for his coming is the life of faith and virtue.

13–14. The use of the present tense for future ('passes' for 'will pass') is not only more vivid but conveys an eternal present: the coming of the Bridegroom is both in time and out of time.

V. 1643–5. The MS. version has the inscription *To the Lady Margaret Ley*. She was the daughter of James Lee (*c.* 1552–1629), a lawyer and statesman who flourished under James I and in the early part of Charles I's reign. After her marriage to one Captain John Hobson in 1641, Margaret Lee lived near Milton in Aldersgate Street, and it seems that he saw much of her after his wife's return to Oxford in 1642.

1–2. James Lee became Lord High Treasurer in 1624, and was created Earl of Marlborough by Charles I; he subsequently became Lord President of the Council, a less important office (and so mentioned first in the sonnet).

3. As Lord Chief Justice in 1622, Lee pronounced sentence on Francis Bacon, who was tried and convicted on charges of corruption.

4, 5–6. Immediately before Lee's death in 1629, Parliament was dissolved by Charles I, after it had challenged his foreign policy and refused to grant him financial support. The King's action was taken in the face of protests and some disorder in the House of Commons, and it marked a breach with the Parliamentary leaders, after which he tried for eleven years to rule without the support of any Parliament. 'It would appear that Milton was told by Lady Margaret herself, in those reminiscences referred to in the sonnet, that the news of these ominous events had hastened her father's end' (Wright). However, the former Lord Treasurer was in his ninety-eighth year when he died.

6–7. At Chaeronea in 338 B.C. the armies of Athens and Thebes were defeated by Philip of Macedon, father of Alexander the Great; Greece then lost its independence and became a part of the Macedonian empire.

8. *that old man eloquent*: the Athenian orator Isocrates, who was said to have died four days after the battle of Chaeronea, at the age of 97. He had exhorted Athens to reform its corrupt politics and re-establish its former democratic integrity, but the Macedonian victory put an end to such hopes.

12–14. The compliment is neatly turned: the old statesman's daughter, devoted to his memory, tells convincing stories of her father's greatness, and in doing so reveals that she has inherited his virtues.

VI. The MS. title is *On the detraction which followed upon my writing certain treatises*. In 1643, a year after his wife returned to her parents, Milton published the first of his tracts on divorce, *The Doctrine and Discipline of Divorce*. His main argument, supported with much biblical and theological learning, was that divorce should be granted not only on the grounds of adultery but also to those who find themselves unsuited to each other in mind and temperament. He considered that in marriage there should be a true intellectual and spiritual companionship: 'a meet and happy conversation is the chiefest and noblest end of marriage'. Milton's advocacy of greater freedom of divorce was received by his contemporaries with great hostility, which surprised and angered him. Not only conventional opinion but many among the Puritans condemned his proposals. It was the opposition of the latter, the party of reform with which he had identified himself, that he felt most bitterly, and that he attacks in this and the next sonnet.

1. *Tetrachordon*, the fourth of the divorce tracts, was published in March 1645. The title is from a Greek word meaning 'four-stringed', referring to a scale-series of four notes; it was meant to suggest that the book had brought into harmony the four chief scriptural passages on marriage and divorce—in Genesis, Deuteronomy, St. Matthew, and First Corinthians. The title would naturally puzzle those who were not learned, like Milton, in both Greek and music.

2. The point made is that the title was related to the contents as carefully as the contents themselves were argued and harmonized.

3–4. 'The subject new' is contrasted with 'now' (when the arguments are no longer new, and the book less read). Milton was not claiming that divorce was a new topic; he himself had been discussing it for nearly two years.

7–8. Mile-End Green was at the eastern limit of London, originally marked by the first milestone on the Roman road to Colchester.

8–9. The struggle between King and Parliament had been precipitated by affairs in Scotland, and the Civil Wars made Englishmen familiar with many Scots names, both of Presbyterian preachers and army leaders. These names 'seemed strange and harsh, and were made more so by mispronunciation and misspelling' (Smart). Milton puts together some such names without intending to ridicule individuals; but he shows already a dislike of the Scottish involvement in English affairs, which comes out fully in Sonnet X.

Colkitto: a Gaelic nickname given to one of the officers of Montrose's army.

Galasp: an English garbling of Gillespie, which may refer to George Gillespie, a Covenanter and member of the Assembly of Divines sitting in London.

11. Quintilian was a classical authority on style; his treatise on oratory gave much attention to the choice of words on grounds of euphony.

12–14. Sir John Cheek (1514–57) was the first Professor of Greek at Cambridge, and tutor to King Edward VI. It has been disputed whether these lines mean that the mid sixteenth century, a period of the revival of learning and of religious reform, was like or *unlike* Milton's own time, whether it hated learning or *not*. Milton is more likely to mean that 'thy age' was as bad as 'ours', and to appeal to Cheek as a fellow scholar, who like himself was hindered by the opinion of his time. Cheek wrote a tract in which he discussed the resistance to the study of Greek: 'The Greek language was hateful to many, and is so now. . . . The good men of the present age abhor the scholarly mind' (Smart).

VII. The MS. title is *On the Same*: the sonnet is again a retort to critics of the divorce tracts, but draws a moral for which Milton was to find a wider application as time went on. Those Puritans who disapproved of his ideas on divorce were hostile also to the freedom of the press which had been established since 1641 by the Long Parliament. In 1643 an Act requiring all publications to be licensed by an official censor was passed by Parliament, now dominated by the Presbyterian party. Milton defied the new Act by publishing his tracts without a licence (he even dedicated a second edition of *The Doctrine and Discipline of Divorce* to the Parliament and the strongly Presbyterian Assembly of Divines). The best known of his prose works followed shortly, *Areopagitica: a Speech for the Liberty of Unlicensed Printing*; it was an attack on censorship, addressed to Parliament. *Areopagitica* was interspersed between divorce tracts, and in this sonnet Milton probably means to include it in his defence of liberty.

1. Note the succession of curt, angry monosyllables, and the deliberately harsh rhyme word.

2. *ancient liberty*: Milton relied on Biblical authority for his proposals on divorce, the laws on which were then based on Canon Law. For the freedom of speech he advocated in *Areopagitica*, he drew examples from ancient Greece and Rome.

4. The birds and animals mentioned had all been given unpleasant associations in literary tradition; the owl represented ignorance, the cuckoo ingratitude, the ass stupidity, the ape silly mockery, the dog quarrelsomeness and slander.

5–7. Latona was loved by Jupiter, and bore him twins, Apollo and Diana. She wandered through the world, fleeing from the wrath of Juno, and in Lycia tried to quench her thirst by drinking from a lake. A band of rustics forbade her, and added insults; as a punishment they were transformed into frogs. Cf. *Arcades*, ll. 20–21 n.

11. 'The distinction between *Liberty* and an irregular and pernicious freedom called *Licence* was familiar to Roman political thought' (Smart). Milton may also intend a sarcastic pun on the kind of 'licence' proposed by his critics, i.e. the licence to be granted before a book could be printed.

12. Milton often repeats this maxim in his later poetry, as a comment on the ultimate failure of the Puritans to establish the free Commonwealth which had been their object.

G

13–14. Cf. the conclusion of Sonnet XI. There is a sudden change of tone, into compassion for the nation's sufferings, which is particularly effective after the fierce scorn of the bulk of the sonnet.

VIII. The sonnet was first published in 1648, among other complimentary poems prefixed to a collection of *Choice Psalms* by Henry Lawes. A copy in the Trinity MS. can be dated early in 1646; it is inscribed *To Mr Henry Lawes on the publishing of his Airs*. Though this title accords well with the contents (l. 8), Lawes did not print the first collection of his Airs until 1653. Lawes was a fervent Royalist, and dedicated his *Choice Psalms* of 1648 to the King, who was then a prisoner awaiting his trial. Milton for his part remained faithful to his friendship with the musician who had been closely associated with some of his finest poetry.

1–4. Lawes was neither the originator nor the sole exemplar of the new style of musical setting for words; but it would have spoilt the compliment if Milton had hedged it round with qualifications. Lawes was certainly a friend to contemporary poets, since he set pieces by Waller, Herrick, Lovelace, Carew, Randolph, and Davenant, as well as Milton; and Waller praised him for the same reason as Milton—that his settings respected and brought out the full meaning of the poetry.

Midas' ears: Midas, King of Phrygia, was the judge in a singing-match between Pan and Apollo, and preferred the piping of Pan. Apollo punished him by giving him ass's ears.

6. *Envy . . . wan*: Envy as an allegorical figure is always depicted with a pale face.

11. *story*: A marginal note in the volume of 1648 tells us that the reference is to Cartwright's *Complaint of Ariadne*, set by Lawes; this has the place of honour in his *Airs and Dialogues* of 1653.

12–14. In the *Purgatorio* (ii. 76–117) Dante meets an old friend, a Florentine musician called Casella, among a crowd of souls newly arrived in Purgatory. Dante addresses him as 'My Casella' (l. 13), and asks him to sing, 'if a new law take not from thee memory or skill in the song of love, which was wont to calm all my desires'. Casella responds by singing one of Dante's *canzoni*, which he had set to music.

milder: The shades of Purgatory are less gloomy than those of Hell.

IX. The MS. heading is *On the religious memory of Mrs Catharine Thomason, my Christian friend, deceased December 1646.* 'Catharine Thomason was the wife of George Thomason, a bookseller and publisher, and a man of knowledge and cultivation. He is remembered for his great collection of some 22,000 pamphlets printed in London during the Civil War and the Commonwealth, which is now in the British Museum and is one of the chief sources of our knowledge of the period. This collection contains several of Milton's tracts, inscribed as given him by the author; and there is other evidence of the friendly association of the two men. Thomason's wife, Catharine, was the niece of Henry Fetherstone, also a well-known bookseller and publisher, to whom Thomason had been originally apprenticed. She was brought up by her uncle, acquiring from him a love of literature and becoming a woman of considerable learning' (Wright). The sonnet has a general resemblance to many Renaissance Italian sonnets on similar occasions (an example by Domenico Mantova is quoted by Smart).

3–4. The idea of earthly life as a form of death separating the soul from God is common in traditional Christianity. Petrarch writes of life as 'questa morte che si chiama vita'.

5. Smart cites 'Thy prayers and alms are come up for a memorial before God' (Acts 10: 4). The sonnet shows that Milton did not hold extreme Protestant views on faith and works.

14. The Book of Revelation has: 'And he shewed me a pure river of water of life, clear as crystal, proceeding out of the throne of God and the Lamb. . . . And let him that is athirst come, and whosoever will, let him take the water of life freely' (20: 1. 17). Cf. *Lycidas*, ll. 174–5.

X. Probably written early in 1646, this sonnet takes further the dislike of Presbyterianism which is reflected in Sonnets VI and VII, and which was the result, not only of Milton's resentment of the reception given to his divorce tracts, but also of developments in the national debate on religion. In 1643 the Long Parliament, having resolved to abolish the Church of England in its episcopal form, set up an Assembly of Divines, and gave it the task of preparing a new constitution for a State Church. The Assembly had only four Scottish members, and about 120 English, but the opinion of the majority proved to be Presbyterian. A group of 'independent' ministers in the Assembly, led by Thomas Goodwin, fought the proposal to set up a Presbyterian Church to which everyone should be made to conform; they upheld the rights of the individual conscience, and advocated a measure of religious toleration. The issue was debated from 1644 to 1646, both in the Assembly and in numerous pamphlets; each side looked to events and persons outside the Assembly to further its cause. The Presbyterians knew that their influence depended on the prowess of the Scottish army fighting on the Parliamentary side; the Independents sought help from Parliament, which was divided, but their main hopes were placed on Cromwell, who was both an Independent and a supporter of toleration.

The form of the sonnet is one often used by the Italians for humorous or satirical subjects; it has a coda or tail, consisting of a half-line (rhyming with the previous line) and a couplet; the coda could be extended indefinitely by adding such units of three lines.

1–2. Episcopacy had been abolished by a vote of Parliament in 1643, and the Anglican liturgy was prohibited, under severe penalties, in 1644. The 'stiff vows' may allude to the Solemn League and Covenant sworn by both Scots and English in 1643.

3–4. 'Pluralism was one of the features of the Anglican church most fiercely attacked by the Puritans. . . . Yet, as Milton repeated several times, no sooner were the Anglican pluralists taken out of their way than the Presbyterians jumped "some into two, some into three, of their best benefices"' (Honigmann). The image of whoredom for pluralism was a Puritan commonplace.

5. 'The Presbyterians demanded that those found guilty of heresy by the Church courts should be punished by the civil magistrate. For blasphemy the penalty was death' (Wright). See Sonnet XIII, l. 12.

7. *classic hierarchy*: Puritans referred to the episcopal form of church government as 'the hierarchy', which thus became a term of abuse. In the system proposed by the English Presbyterians a parish or congregation would be in charge of a minister and ruling elders; ten or twelve congregations would be grouped in a Presbytery or *Classis*. A 'classic hierarchy' mockingly points to the similarity between the episcopal and Presbyterian disciplines (cf. l. 20).

8. *mere A. S.* 'Mere A. S.' was Dr. Adam Stuart, a Scotsman by birth, who had spent some time on the Continent, appeared in London for a few years to take part in the pamphlet warfare, and returned to the Continent in 1644, where he became Professor of Philosophy at Leyden. Stuart wrote against the Independents, and Milton echoes the indignation of one of their pamphlets that 'this one single simple A. S. now starts up by himself, peremptorily to state, and determine the Questions, for the resolution whereof the Parliament thought the Assembly of Divines few enough' (Honigmann).

Rotherford: Samuel Rutherford, Professor of Divinity at St. Andrews, was one of the Scottish members of the Assembly of Divines, and during its deliberations published two treatises advocating Presbyterianism. In 1649 he brought out a *Free Disputation against Pretended Liberty of Conscience*, in which he advocated the death penalty for heresy.

9–12. These lines refer to the five Independent members of the Assembly, who were attacked in publications by the Presbyterians. Thomas Edwards was a preacher in London, who replied to an *Apologetical Narration* by the five Independents, in a work entitled *Antapologia* (1644). 'Scotch What-d'ye-call' has been identified as Robert Baillie, the only Scotch Commissioner in the Assembly; he was openly bitter about the Independents, while acknowledging their learning and piety. Both Edwards and Baillie also attacked Milton for his divorce tracts at about this time.

14. The Church of Rome reacted to the Reformation by convening the Council of Trent (1545–63), which redefined Roman Catholic doctrine and established a more effective discipline in the Church. The new order was not evolved without much political manœuvring, and the Council was execrated by Protestants.

15. In looking to Parliament to check the Presbyterian attempt to impose uniformity, Milton was appealing to a body of diverse opinions; no one could know what party would prevail, but Parliament had already shown some disapproval of the claims to authority made by the Assembly of Divines. The Presbyterians continued to be powerful in the House of Commons, even after the defeat of the Scots by Cromwell in 1648; but Cromwell's rise to supreme power gave ascendancy to the Independents.

17. Phylacteries were slips of vellum inscribed with quotations from the Mosaic Law, which were worn by pious Jews on their foreheads, as badges of sanctity. Christ refers to them in denouncing the Pharisees: 'But all their works they do for to be seen of men; they make broad their phylacteries. . . .' (Matt. 23: 5). 'The whole line means: that the Parliament may abate your pharisaical pretensions, though they do not (as the Star-Chamber would have done) cut off your ears' (Worrall). When Laud was Archbishop of Canterbury, Puritan propagandists ran the risk of having their ears cropped. An earlier version of this sonnet referred here to William Prynne, a Puritan whose ears were cut off in 1634, as a punishment for criticisms of the King and Queen in his *Histriomastix*. But Prynne, though a Presbyterian, was opposed to the Assembly's demands for uniformity, and Milton may have removed his name for this reason.

20. It was a common accusation at the time that the Presbyterian system was as rigid as the Roman Catholic, implying 'a pope in every parish'. Milton gives magnificent expression to the charge by using his awareness of etymology.

XI. MS. title: *On the Lord General Fairfax at the siege of Colchester*. Colchester surrendered on 27 August 1648, but the sonnet must have been written before news came of Cromwell's defeat of the Scots (l. 7) at Preston on August 17. Sir Thomas Fairfax (1612–71) decided the outcome of the First Civil War by his victories at Marston Moor (1644) and Naseby (1645); by 1646 the Royalist party was powerless throughout England, and two years of peace followed. But the Second Civil War began in 1648, with the outbreak of concerted Royalist rebellions in various parts of the country, and an invasion by the Scots (ll. 6–8). Cromwell led the forces of the Parliament against the Royalists in South Wales, and after defeating them, marched north to meet the Scots. Fairfax was in command of the forces meeting the rebellion in the South and East. He drove the Royalists out of Kent, but some crossed the Thames to join those who had risen in Essex, and based their resistance on Colchester. Fairfax besieged it, until famine and the defeat of the Royalists elsewhere forced it to surrender. Though Fairfax stayed on as Commander-in-Chief, power passed into the hands of Cromwell and Ireton. 'He had no direct share in the condemnation of

Charles, whom he would have spared, had it been in his power, but hesitated and acquiesced. In the following year [1650] he retired from his command, and withdrew into private life' (Smart).

Milton addresses Fairfax as a great commander whom he exhorts to show himself a great statesman. Yet the sonnet was written just when Fairfax began to lose what political importance he had, though he had attained the height of his success as a general.

This and three other sonnets (XII, XIII, XVIII) were not printed as Milton's until 1694, twenty years after his death: doubtless because they all relate to heroic figures and events of the Commonwealth period.

7. *Hydra*: See *Comus*, l. 605 n.

7–8. *the false North . . . league*: The Scottish army, under the Duke of Hamilton, marched into England to support the Royalists in July 1648. Scotland and the Parliament had been united in their resistance to Charles since 1643, by the Solemn League and Covenant.

12–14. Accusations of fraud, avarice, and rapine were at this time being brought by the Independents and their army supporters against the Parliament and its Presbyterian committees. In a passage added to his *History of Britain*, Milton denounces the councils and committees that 'fell to huckster the commonwealth; men for the most part of insatiable hands and noted disloyalty; the ravening seizure of innumerable thieves in office'. The opportunities for such malpractices had come with the Civil War; in order to raise funds for the prosecution of the war, the Parliament resorted to confiscation. The estates of Royalists were declared forfeit, and either sold, or bought back by the owners on payment of a proportion of their value. 'In the enforced sale of Royalist estates it became possible to make purchases at low rates by official connivance; and Royalists who sought to make terms sometimes found it necessary to smooth the way by judicious bribery. Property was thus changing hands in every part of England, with many circumstances of distress and impoverishment, rapacity and extortion. Adherents of the Parliament did not escape, but complained bitterly. . . .' (Smart).

12. *public faith*: 'Initially *public faith* meant simply "national honour". But in Milton's day the phrase was widely used to refer to a form of National Debt incurred by the Parliament' (Honigmann).

XII. The Committee for the Propagation of the Gospel was appointed by Parliament in the spring of 1652, in yet another attempt to settle the state of religion in England. The ministers whose proposals Milton disliked were Independents, among them being some of those five members of the Assembly whom he had praised in 1646 (see Sonnet X, ll. 9-12). They were now proposing to set up an Established Church, and concerned with the limits of toleration to be allowed to religious teaching outside it. In their discussions with the Parliamentary Committee, they suggested that such religious teaching should only be allowed in public, and with the consent of the civil authorities; a later condition proposed was that 'no one should be permitted to speak in public of any religious question without a certificate from two or more godly and orthodox ministers, attesting his sufficiency to speak and soundness in the faith' (Smart). They had also recommended that no one should be allowed to speak against the fundamental principles of the Christian religion, and produced a list of fifteen points defining these. Milton was indignant at what appeared to him a new threat to freedom of conscience, and appealed to Cromwell as the supreme power in the country, and one who was known to be firmly opposed to intolerance. In the three years which had passed since Milton wrote Sonnet XI, he had proved himself a powerful defender of Cromwell's policies, and he was also Secretary for Foreign Tongues. He was not a member of the Government, and had no special influence on Cromwell. Nevertheless the sonnet is intended, not only to encourage Cromwell by its praise but to admonish him to resist intolerance in the guise of a State Church.

2. *detractions rude*: Cromwell's astonishing rise to almost royal power naturally roused mistrust and envy.

5-6. 'The idea is that the servant of the true God has triumphed over the pagan Goddess of Fortune' (Wright). But 'crownèd Fortune' is also an allusion to the monarchy, and 'neck' is a clear reference to Cromwell's responsibility for the execution of Charles I. Cf. Joshua 10: 24, 'put your feet upon the necks of these kings'. Line 5 was omitted even in 1694.

7. *Darwen*: a small stream that flows into the Ribble at Preston, where Cromwell routed the Scots invaders in 1648.

8. Cromwell defeated the Scots at Dunbar in 1650.

9. At the battle of Worcester in 1651 Cromwell achieved his crowning victory, when he defeated a Scottish army led by Charles II.

13-14. Cf. *Lycidas*, ll. 114-22. 'The comparison of corrupt ministers with wolves is biblical in origin (Acts 20: 29: "after my departing shall grievous wolves enter in among you")' (Honigmann).

XIII. Sir Henry Vane (1613-62) was one of the ablest Parliamentary leaders, who had made himself an expert on foreign affairs, as well as being deeply versed in religious issues. He had consistently advocated toleration, both in Parliament and as a member of the Assembly of Divines (where Milton had often attended to hear him speak). In 1649 he joined Cromwell's Council of State, and at the time the sonnet was written (July 1652), he had just been engaged in difficult negotiations with the Dutch. There had been for some time a crisis in the relations between Holland and England, and war had been declared when Milton wrote his poem. The Dutch had the largest merchant navy in Europe, and England had begun to challenge Holland for the supremacy of the sea. Dutch ambassadors were sent to England at the end of 1651, but were suspected of protracting negotiations for their own purposes, rather than seeking peace. There was an encounter between the English and Dutch fleets in May 1652, and Vane took charge of intensive discussions with the Dutch ambassadors in June. Vane forced matters to a conclusion by challenging the good faith of the Dutch; it is clear from the sonnet that he was thought to have successfully penetrated their motives, and Milton may have helped him to do so (see Honigmann, pp. 156-7). 'These events are referred to by Milton in the first half of his sonnet, a copy of which he sent to Vane three days after the ambassadors were dismissed. The latter part of the poem presents Vane as a champion of Milton's own views on religious toleration' (Wright). In thus moving from political to spiritual concerns Milton follows a familiar pattern, and brings the poem to a calm and generous conclusion.

1. *young in years*: Vane was nearly forty in 1652, but he had commonly been called the younger Sir Henry Vane; his father, who bore the same name, was still alive.

2–3. The comparison between the English Parliament and the Roman Senate was obvious, and made a special appeal to Milton.

3–4. Much was due to the wisdom and courage of the Roman Senate in Rome's victorious resistance to the invasions of Pyrrhus, King of Epirus (280–272 B.C.), and Hannibal (220–182 B.C.).

6. *hollow states*: a punning allusion to the States-General of Holland, whose intentions Vane had been trying to penetrate.

8. It was a common saying that money was the sinews of war, but Machiavelli in his *Discorsi* (ii 10—a passage Milton read at about this time) argued that 'war is made with iron, not with gold' (Honigmann).

9–12. The distinction between authority in spiritual matters and civil authority was the basis of Milton's mature thought. If any authority was to be recognized in religious questions, it should be left in the hands of 'the faithful', to be exercised among themselves. In the *Defence of the English People* Milton wrote: 'Men at first united in civil society that they might live in safety and freedom, without suffering violence and wrong, in the Church that they might live in religion and holiness. The one has its laws, and the other its discipline, which is utterly different'.

which few have done: 'Milton probably means that few other *senators*, or politicians, have studied the relationship of civil and spiritual authority, for the subject was of course much discussed by theologians' (Honigmann).

either sword: '. . . it was possible to speak of the *spiritual sword* in a purely emblematic fashion, without suggesting constraint or compulsion by any kind of force' (Smart).

14. *eldest son*: main support of a parent.

XIV. The Vaudois or Valdenses were regarded after the Reformation as the earliest Protestants, having been condemned by the Church in 1215; they taught the virtues of poverty, self-denial, and a simple Christian faith. Their origins were obscure, and in Milton's time they were popularly thought to go back to Apostolic times; but it is now accepted that they began as a movement within the Church, and were founded by Pierre Valdes, a merchant of Lyons. Adherents of the sect were to be found in certain valleys of the Alps, on the borders of France and Italy, where they were protected by the terrain and by the absence, for many centuries, of any powerful authority. After the Reformation they were organized into a Protestant church, under the influence of Geneva.

In 1655 Europe was shocked by a brutal massacre of those Vaudois living in the territory of the Duke of Savoy, in the valleys of the Pellice and the Angrogna, in Piedmont. The inhabitants of these valleys had been granted toleration in 1561 by a treaty with the Duke of that time; but the terms excluded them from some villages in the lower valleys, into which they subsequently spread. 'In January 1655 an edict was issued commanding all those Vaudois living outside the prescribed limits to withdraw; in April an army was sent to enforce the order, whereupon the Vaudois in these districts fled to their fellow religionists in the hills. The district was now cleared of the offending Vaudois and the treaty of 1651 vindicated; but the Duke had evidently resolved to exterminate the sect. On 24 April his army attacked the villages in the tolerated area, laying them waste; men, women, and children were all put to the sword, and many of those who escaped over the Alps towards the French frontier perished in the snow' (Wright).

Cromwell regarded himself as the champion of Protestantism in Europe, and made great exertions to organize and make effective the indignation which was felt in all Protestant countries. Milton composed many of the letters in which Cromwell voiced his protest and proposed intervention: a letter was sent to the Duke of Savoy, urging religious toleration; others went to the Kings of Sweden and Denmark, the Dutch Republic, and the Protestant Cantons of Switzerland, inviting them to make their own representations; France was asked to join in protesting. These dispatches made it plain that Cromwell did not intend to confine himself to diplomacy, if force should prove to be necessary; the English navy might have landed troops on the Duke's territory, on the coast which we now call the Italian Riviera. Meanwhile the Vaudois, who had been taken by surprise in the massacre, rallied in their own defence; and they defeated the Piedmontese troops in the fighting which followed. In August the Duke of Savoy made peace with them, restoring their ancient rights.

1. Smart quotes: 'And when he had opened the fifth seal, I saw under the altar the souls of them that were slain for the word of God, and for the testimony which they held: And they cried with a

loud voice, saying, How long, O Lord, holy and true, dost thou not judge and avenge our blood on them that dwell on the earth' (Rev. 6: 9–10).

saints: Puritans called all true believers saints, in accordance with both the Old and the New Testaments.

4. Like the Israelites in the Old Testament, Puritans rejected all religious images and statues as idolatrous: cf. '[Israel] defiled the land, and committed adultery with stones and with stocks' (Jer. 3: 9).

6. 'Not only an allusion to the biblical commonplace about God's sheep and the good shepherd: Milton also echoes the Psalmist's cry that the children of God must be prepared for persecution and slaughter: "Yea, for thy sake are we killed all the day long; we are counted as sheep for the slaughter" (44: 22 . . .)' (Honigmann).

7–10. Honigmann observes that 'the description and attitudes of the sonnet' reproduce those of contemporary news-letters, from which he quotes passages that would have been read by Milton and his fellow Londoners.

10–13. Tertullian was perhaps the first to assert that 'the blood of the martyrs is the seed of the Church'.

12. *The triple Tyrant*: the Pope, whose tiara has three crowns.

14. In one of Petrarch's invectives against the Papal Court, he calls it a 'fountain of woe' and 'a false and wicked Babylon'. The Church of Rome was identified by the Puritans with the symbolic Babylon whose destruction is foretold in Revelation (17, 18).

XV. Milton became totally blind early in 1652. His sight had been failing since about 1644, and the left eye was blind by the beginning of 1650. He was then warned by his physicians that he risked losing his sight completely if he continued to work intensively. But in January 1650 the Council of State asked him to reply to the attack made by Salmasius on the English republicans, and he chose to accept the task, with the result that his physicians predicted (see Sonnet XVIII). Scholars have differed in their views of when the sonnet was written; but the importance of assigning a date within two or three years after 1652 has been exaggerated. The order in which Milton printed the sonnets is roughly chronological, and this follows *On the late Massacre*, indicating that it may not have been written until 1655. But to give it such a date would pair it with Sonnet XVIII, which expresses a rather different feeling towards his blindness. A literal reading of 'ere half my days' would push the date back to 1644 or earlier, when Milton's sight was only vaguely threatened; and would deprive the sonnet of its justification. It has been argued that Milton would not feel that his 'talent' was 'useless' while he was engaged in major works of controversy. But by *one* talent he must have meant that of poetry; and while he knew from experience that blindness did not prevent him from producing prose or doing other official work, he might well have wondered whether he would ever be able now to compose the great poem which had always been his ambition. The thoughts and emotions of the sonnet need not be attributed to a passing mood, or to one datable occasion, a day, a month, or a year. The poem must be taken to represent an early reaction to total blindness; but Milton may have found the perfect expression for this only after a year or two. We can find parallels to the shape and adjustment of his feelings here in poems as widely separated as *Lycidas* and *Samson Agonistes*. The sonnet is one example of the way in which Milton as a poet repeatedly met misfortune, doubt, and discouragement.

2. *Ere half my days*: Milton was forty-three in 1652, and scholars have worried over the supposed implication that he assumed a life-span of eighty-six. But for many years Milton seems to have felt, as he looked, younger than he was; and he calls Vane 'young in years' at the age of forty. There are other expressions in the sonnets which raise difficulties if taken too literally; see Sonnet XIX, l. 7.

3-6. In Matthew 25: 14 ff., the servant who receives one talent of money in trust from his Lord buries it, and can show no increase when the Lord returns; while those who received five and two talents traded with those sums and doubled them. The servant who hid his talent is severely rebuked, and punished by having it taken away. In a letter associated with Sonnet II, Milton refers to 'the terrible seizing of him that hid the talent', in connection with his responsibility for the proper use of his gift for poetry.

4. *useless*: has not only its ordinary meaning, but a play of words on 'use' as 'usury', earning interest.

7. *day-labour*: labour hired or measured by the day.

11. *yoke*: Cf. Matt. 11: 29–30: 'Take my yoke upon you, and learn of me . . . For my yoke is easy, and my burden is light.'

14. In many passages of the Old and the New Testaments 'wait' is used of patience, devotion, and submission to God: cf. 'Wait on the Lord: be of good courage, and he shall strengthen thine heart: wait, I say, on the Lord' (Psalms, 27: 14).

XVI. This and the following sonnet are social invitations in the manner of Horace. They are addressed to younger men who cultivated Milton's friendship during the years when he was living in a 'pretty garden-house in Petty-France in Westminster' (1652–60); despite his blindness, this period must have given Milton much satisfaction, in the fame which his Latin writings had brought him throughout Europe, and its social consequences.

The father and son of l. 1 were Henry Lawrence, who was Lord President of Cromwell's Council, and his elder son Edward (1633–57). Edward Lawrence was a young man of exceptional ability and promise, who had been taken abroad at an early age, and had much of his education in Germany and Holland. He was versed in languages, and had scientific and philosophical interests; Milton speaks to him as one sharing his own cultivated and cosmopolitan tastes (ll. 9–12). Lawrence became a Member of Parliament at the age of twenty-three, and seemed destined for success in public life; but he died in 1657, which may not have been long after Milton sent him this invitation.

1–3. Milton has in mind walks taken with Lawrence in good weather; to help him to exercise in this way may have been one of the services performed by his younger friends.

6. Horace invokes Favonius in an invitation to Sestius to enjoy the delights of spring (*Odes*, II. iv).

8. 'Consider the lilies of the field, how they grow; they toil not, neither do they spin' (Matt. 6: 28).

10. *Of Attic taste*: The Athenians, even in their feasts, liked simplicity and restraint.

13–14. 'This passage has sometimes been taken as equivalent to "spare time to interpose them oft", i.e. indulge in them freely; but this is a forced construction, and contradicts the Horatian sentiment of moderation which we should look for in so Horatian a poem'

(Smart). Some recent critics have tried to restore the meaning rejected by Smart, bringing what they consider to be new evidence from the *Disticha Catonis*, iii. 7. Milton had always stressed the need and the value of such recreations as music; but here he aims at balance, in his recommendation of them. Having so far presented the evening's pleasures as straightforwardly enjoyable, if refined and simple, he wishes to end on a more thoughtful note. A man may be considered wise, he says, if he can do two things, which are really the same thing: 'judge', i.e. be judicious about, such delights, which means both to enjoy them and to value them rightly; and *consequently*, 'spare' to indulge in them too much, i.e. show his judiciousness in practice.

XVII. Cyriack Skinner (1627–1700) was the grandson of Sir Edward Coke, once Chief Justice of the King's Bench, and the greatest jurist of his time. Like his grandfather, Skinner became a lawyer, and was admitted to membership of Lincoln's Inn in 1647. He was said to have been 'scholar to John Milton', and may have been one of the pupils Milton took in his house in Aldersgate Street. Certainly he remained a devoted friend, and gave Milton practical help at the time of the Restoration. A letter from Marvell in the summer of 1654 tells us that Skinner had lately come to be a near-neighbour of Milton; there is no reason to think that he did not visit the poet regularly before this, but the sonnet (which is probably earlier than Sonnet XVIII, in view of the more formal opening) may have been written about then.

2. *British Themis*: the English system of law. Themis was the Greek Goddess of Justice.

3. The notice 'To the Reader' in Coke's *Certain Select Cases* (1659) says that Coke's 'Person in his life time was reverenced as an Oracle, and his Works (since his decease) cyted as Authentick Authorities, even by the Reverend Judges themselves' (Honigmann). Coke's *Reports* and *Institutes of the Laws of England* are legal classics.

7. Euclid (*c*. 300 B.C.) and Archimedes (287?–212 B.C.) were Greek geometers, who would have been studied by Milton's pupils. They represent 'the science of measuring', and this is contrasted with the art of measuring *life* in l. 9.

8. *the Swede*: This was a not uncommon way of referring to a

country, as 'the Dane' for Denmark, 'the Spaniard' for Spain.
Probably both the mode of description and choice of country are
influenced by the military success of Charles X of Sweden, who
succeeded to the throne in 1654, and initiated a campaign against
Poland. 'But England was negotiating treaties with both Sweden
and France a little earlier, in 1653–4, and both negotiations ran into
difficulties. *The Swede* could refer to the Sweden of Queen Christina,
and *the French* to the slippery France of Mazarin before or after
1654' (Honigmann). More important than a precise reference is the
plain echo of Horace's advice (*Odes*, II, xi), to enjoy present happiness and 'to cease from enquiring what the warlike Cantabrian and
the Scythians intend'.

XVIII. Like the two which precede it, this sonnet is evidence of the
relative calm and content which came to Milton in the mid 1650s.
The year in which the poem was written, 1655, he published the
Defensio Pro Se, in which, after having confounded his country's
enemies with the two *Defences of the English People* (1651, 1654), he
answered the personal attacks made on him in the course of the
controversy. Sonnet XV shows him submitting the riddle of his
blindness to patience, and waiting on the will of God; there is no
reference to active work or hope. The present sonnet both looks
back on a great achievement and looks forward (ll. 8–9) to continued exertion. The poem may indeed record a momentous
turning-point, when he could give up official duties and return to
poetry. In 1655 his salary was commuted to a life pension, having
been reduced when his blindness made it necessary for him to have
an assistant Latin Secretary (1652). The literary tasks he now took
up (the *History of Britain*, the *Christian Doctrine*) can be seen as
preparations for the great national and religious epic he had had to
postpone since 1641.

1. *this three years' day*: This idiom means 'for three years', and does
not imply an anniversary of the day in 1652 on which Milton
became completely blind.

1–2. Writing of his blindness in the *Second Defence* (1654), Milton
says that 'to external appearance' his eyes 'are as completely without
injury, as clear and bright, without the semblance of a cloud, as the
eyes of those whose sight is the most perfect'.

7–9. 'In a letter to Henry Oldenburg of 6 July 1654, Milton said that having vindicated Liberty he would prepare himself for "other labours ... An idle ease has never had charms for me" ' (Honigmann).

10–13. i.e. in writing the *Defence of the English People* (1651). See Sonnet XV.

14. *had I no better guide*: implies that his religious faith would have been enough to support him, even without the thought of his work for freedom.

XIX. Until modern scholars raised an inconclusive debate on the question, this sonnet was generally taken to refer to Milton's second wife, Katherine Woodcock, whom he married in 1656, and who died in February 1658. The placing of the poem indicates a date after 1655. Not only the sentiment, but several details, seem appropriate to Katherine Woodcock; but it has been argued that everything in the poem could apply equally well, or better, to Mary Powell, Milton's first wife, who died in 1652.—Katherine Woodcock was born in London in 1628; her father and grandfather had ranked as country gentlemen, but had dissipated their resources. Fortunately her mother had well-to-do relations in London, who helped her. Katherine was 28 when Milton married her, and it appears from the sonnet that he had not met her until after he became blind (l. 10). She died in giving birth to a daughter in October 1657, the child surviving her only a few weeks.—A vision or dream of a dead wife or lover is the subject of many Italian sonnets.

1. *late espousèd*: This can mean either 'the woman I lately married' or 'my wife lately dead'. If Katherine Woodcock is intended, it could mean *both*.

saint: a soul in heaven. 'In one of the poems of Bembo, lamenting the death of his lady, he addresses her as *santa*' (Smart).

2–4. 'In the tragedy of Euripides, Alcestis gives her life as a ransom for that of her husband; but Hercules, "the son of Zeus", wrestles with death and brings Alcestis back from the grave' (Wright).

5–6. Under the Mosaic Law women had to undergo ritual purification after child-birth (Lev. 12: 5). The lines have been said to imply that the dead wife had not undergone purification; and while Katherine Woodcock survived childbirth long enough to have done so, Mary Powell did not. But Milton does not mean to indicate any particular lapse of time, but only that his wife had died after bearing a child, and that she was pure in both body and mind.

7-8. 'Once more' has been interpreted as meaning that Milton had seen his wife's face in real life, and this would seem to exclude Katherine Woodcock; but it refers more probably to the glimpse of her he has in the dream, since this is not (as in Heaven it will be) 'without restraint'; and the next lines tell us why.

9. *Her face was veil'd*: 'The allusion to a veiled face has been traced to a passage in the *Alcestis*; but in the tragedy Alcestis is not recognized by her husband when her face is covered, and is treated by him as a stranger until the veil is removed. Milton recognizes his wife in spite of the veil. It is clear that he alludes to his blindness during their married life' (Smart).

13. *inclined*: 'The dream seems to melt into reality at this point: in the moment between sleeping and waking Milton is conscious of lying in his bed, and his dream lingers long enough for his *Saint* to appear to see him there' (Honigmann).

14. *day brought back my night*: His 'night' is both blindness and bereavement. Like the statement that he knew his wife's face was veiled, the image implies that in his dream he had the illusion of sight.

Renaissance Platonism and Cosmology

(i)

HAVING joined in religious controversy in 1641, Milton soon found himself being slandered in scurrilous terms by his opponents. He replied by introducing into his ecclesiastical pamphlets some passages giving an account of his life and poetic vocation. One of these passages, printed in 1642, defends him against the charge of moral corruption, and may serve to introduce the subject of his Platonism. Speaking apparently of his boyhood, Milton says:

... I betook me among those lofty Fables and Romances, which recount in solemne canto's the deeds of Knighthood founded by our victorious Kings; and from hence had in renowne over all Christendome. There I read it in the oath of every Knight, that he should defend to the expence of his best blood, or of his life, if it so befell him, the honour and chastity of Virgin or Matron. From whence even then I learnt what a noble vertue chastity sure must be, to the defence of which so many worthies by such a deare adventure of themselves had sworne.... Only this my minde gave me that every free and gentle spirit without that oath ought to be borne a Knight, nor needed to expect the guilt spurre, or the laying of a sword upon his shoulder to stirre him up both by his counsell, and his arme to secure and protect the weaknesse of any attempted chastity. ...

Thus from the Laureat fraternity of Poets, riper yeares, and the ceaselesse round of study and reading led me to the shady spaces of philosophy, but chiefly to the divine volumes of *Plato*, and his equall *Xenophon*. Where if I should tell ye what I learnt, of chastity and love, I meane that which is truly so, whose charming cup is only vertue which she bears in her hand to those who are worthy. The rest are cheated with a thick intoxicating potion which a certaine Sorceresse the abuser of loves name carries about; and how the first and chiefest office of love, begins and ends in the soule, producing those happy twins of her divine generation knowledge and vertue, with such abstracted sublimities as these, it might be worth your listning. . . .[1]

He goes on to say that a Christian education alone would have made clear, to one of his temperament, the importance of sexual purity. But the stress on Platonism, as 'the noblest Philosophy', is a key to all the poetry of his youth.

As a Greek scholar, Milton of course read Plato (427?–347 B.C.) in the original. But we cannot understand his interpretation of Platonic philosophy unless we recognize the influence on Renaissance poets of the revived Platonism of the fifteenth century Florentine Academy, and especially of its founder, Marsilio Ficino (1433–99).

The central tenet of Plato's philosophy, as interpreted by Ficino, is that the soul is immortal, and can only attain happiness by ascending from attachment to bodily things to the knowledge and love of God. Knowledge of truth and love of the good are vital to the ascent; but the soul learns how to reach God chiefly through human love and friendship, to which Ficino gives the name of Platonic love. The importance of Plato's doctrine of the soul to Milton is apparent in Comus.[2]

It was the Italian humanists of the fifteenth century who made possible, through their study of Greek, the new Platonism of the Renaissance. Ficino's translation made Plato's complete works available for the first time to Western Europe. The immediate result was an attempt by

[1] An Apology for Smectymnuus.
[2] See Commentary, p. 135.

some to substitute Platonism for Aristotelianism, as the dominant philosophy in the Church, and by others to reconcile the two. But the New Learning was on the whole hostile to the medieval scholastic philosophy founded on Aristotle; and the revival of Plato contributed to its overthrow, and eventually to the Reformation. The attempt to replace Aristotle by Plato was rendered easier by the fact that, in the early centuries of Christianity, the Platonic tradition had been absorbed into the thought of the Church Fathers, and had been a decisive influence on Saint Augustine (A.D. 354–430).

The Renaissance Platonists set out to make a new synthesis between religion and philosophy; the materials at their disposal included late Platonic and pseudo-Platonic writings, as well as those of Plato himself. Ficino and his followers regarded the Platonic tradition as a non-Christian parallel to the revelation of God in the Old and the New Testaments. They were led to this view particularly by their inclusion in it of a mass of mystical, pseudo-scientific, and magical treatises attributed to one Hermes Trismegistus (the 'thrice great Hermes' of *Il Penseroso*, l. 88). When these Hermetic writings were discovered, Ficino hastened to translate them, in 1463, even before he had translated the works of Plato. We now know that the Hermetic writings belong to the second and third centuries A.D.; but they claimed to transmit Egyptian wisdom of immemorial antiquity, and the Renaissance scholars accepted their claim. Hermes Trismegistus was supposed to be a semi-divine prophetic teacher, and was identified both with Mercury, the messenger of the Gods, and with the Egyptian God Thoth. The works attributed to him contained echoes of Mosaic religion and Platonic speculation. Not realizing that these parallels had been taken into the

Hermetic works from the floating synthetic mysticism of the late classical period, Ficino and his followers thought they proved that Hermes had something of the authority of the Jewish religion, and had perhaps inspired Plato.

While we now regard the mystical and magical Hermetic philosophy as confused and incoherent, and alien to both Platonism and Christianity, it undoubtedly gave an added excitement to Renaissance art and speculation. In its time it was a stimulus to scientific theory and experiment, being mixed with the doctrines of alchemy; and it persisted as an undercurrent in Christian mysticism—for example, in the poetry of Henry Vaughan (?1621–95). Milton accepts Hermeticism as a part of the Platonic heritage in *Il Penseroso* (ll. 85–96 and 170–4); but the tone of the poem should tell us that he takes its secret lore as material for poetic fancy, not as serious thought.

(ii)

The Renaissance Platonist synthesis was important for art and poetry because it gave a new perspective on the whole development of civilization as then understood, and gave a new significance to classical culture in particular. All ancient art, religion, and literature could be assumed to have a hidden meaning—always the same meaning, no doubt, since it was a premonition or a symbol of Christian truth. This theory was formulated by Pico Della Mirandola (1463–1494), and in so far as it concerned classical mythology, it remained the orthodox approach throughout the sixteenth and earlier seventeenth centuries. It can be traced throughout Spenser's *Faerie Queene*, it underlies Ben Jonson's Masques, and it appears in a surprising context in Francis Bacon's *Wisdom of the Ancients* (1609). At the same time, while Spenser and Milton after him represent this more or less philosophical interpretation of classical myth, many Elizabethan and other English poets exploited the myths merely for their sensuous or imaginative beauty. Thus Marlowe in *Hero and Leander* uses the classical gods to represent a life of superhuman sensual freedom. But Spenser turns classical legends into moral allegory. His Acrasia and her Bower of Bliss (*The Faerie Queene*, Book Two) go back, through Italian poetry, to Circe. The loves of Venus and Adonis become a symbol of perpetual fertility and decay in Nature in the Gardens of Adonis (Book Three); and the Three Graces are absorbed into an allegory of poetry, love, and courtesy, revealed in a throng of naked maidens dancing to a shepherd's pipe on Mount Acidale (Book Six).

The use of mythology by Spenser and Milton in fact reflects the dual nature of Renaissance culture, in its variable combination of classical and Christian elements. Milton's strictest control over the hidden meaning of classical myths comes in his mature poetry, and above all in *Paradise Lost*, where every allusion is integrated into his view of world history and of God's dealings with Man. The classical myths are there seen in relation to the Old Testament, and to the Book of Genesis in particular. The Greek fables of wars between Titans, Gods, and giants are parallels to the revolt of Satan and the consequent War in Heaven; the rape of Proserpine by Pluto is associated with Eve's deception by the serpent; the Garden of the Hesperides and the Golden Age are linked with Eden and Man's life before the Fall. There is an underlying assumption that the collective memory of mankind had preserved some outline of the true events (i.e. those ultimately revealed in the Bible), and that the classical legends were garbled versions based on those memories.

In the earlier poetry Milton's view is not so uniform or so logical. It varies between a religious point of view which is fundamentally the same as in *Paradise Lost*, and is to be seen in the Nativity Ode; and the more relaxed, almost Elizabethan delight in the artistic resources of mythology, which appears in *Comus* and *Lycidas*. Even in those poems, however, the poet's method is essentially allegorical. It may be useful to trace the outlines of these variations.

Milton was already an accomplished Latin poet when he wrote his first important poem in English, the Nativity Ode. His poetic exercises and experiments, both as a schoolboy and as an undergraduate, had been mostly in Latin, and the writing of Latin verse demanded an expert knowledge of Greek and Roman mythology. Dr. Johnson is pointing to this obvious aspect of classical studies when, sneering at *Lycidas*, he refers to the appearance in it of 'the heathen deities—Jove and Phoebus, Neptune and Æolus, with a long train of mythological imagery, such as a college easily supplies'. Milton's Fifth Latin Elegy, written when he was twenty, shows both his skill and his intense pleasure in the imaginary world of the pagan gods. In this poem the coming of spring is celebrated by the Olympians and all the powers of the earth, with love and feasting; the myths dramatize the drunken joy and desire of Nature. The poem has a sensuous abandonment such as Milton never put into his English verse, and which he can only express in Latin because then he is free to use the mythological dream-world, as a part of a literary convention. Writing in English, however, he must use mythology, if at all, as a part of a modern and rational view of life.

His first attempt, in the Nativity Ode, is almost narrowly theological: the Graeco-Roman religions are the work of demons, fallen spirits which deceived men before Christ brought them the truth. The inevitable result of this doctrine, which goes back to the Church Fathers, is that the really evil and cruel religions denounced in the Old Testament are emphasized at the expense of the Greek and Roman cults (and this emphasis is repeated even more plainly in *Paradise Lost*, Book I).

But when Milton set out to develop his powers as an English poet, he put aside explicitly religious themes for a time, and turned as a pupil to the varied Elizabethan poetic inheritance. We can trace his reading of Marlowe, Shakespeare, Ben Jonson, and Spenser, and see him learning from what they had done with classical myths. This might be called 'the mythological period' of his poetry, running from *L'Allegro* and *Il Penseroso* to *Comus*; and it is permeated with allegory of the Renaissance Platonist kind. When the religious theme emerges again, in *Lycidas*, it can wield a poetry vastly enriched by the lessons of the preceding five years or so; but there is a more personal and passionate seriousness in *Lycidas*, which seems to exclude the leisurely half-playful allegorizing of *Comus*.

(iii)

A new theory of the universe emerged in the Renaissance, formulated by Copernicus (1543): the sun was at the centre, and the earth and other planets revolved round it. But in Milton's time the new cosmology had not yet won general acceptance. Even in *Paradise Lost*, composed in the latter half of the century, he used the old system, though he indicated that it might well be superseded by that of Copernicus and Galileo. So, too, in all his earlier poetry he makes use of the old cosmology, the Ptolemaic universe, which was an integral part of medieval culture.

In the universe as described in the second century A.D.

by Ptolemy, who followed other Greek astronomers and mathematicians, the earth stood fixed at the centre, and the stars and the planets circled round it. Their motions were explained as the result of revolving spheres concentric to the earth. Each of the seven 'planets' had its sphere; all the fixed stars were located in another sphere, the Eighth Heaven. Ascending from the earth, one came first to the sphere of the moon, next to those of Mercury, Venus, the sun, Mars, Jupiter, and Saturn, in that order; the sphere of the fixed stars came next, and the whole was enclosed by the sphere of the First Mover, or *Primum Mobile*, which imparted movement to all the eight spheres below it.

The Ptolemaic model of the universe was recognized to be not wholly adequate, and medieval and later astronomers added to it, or modified it, in order to account more completely for the observed phenomena. But centuries of thought and imagination and observation went into the construction and presentation of the system; literature of all kinds used it, and modern scholars have shown how important it is to our understanding of European culture down to the late Renaissance. And though the Renaissance brought new speculations and an increased knowledge of the physical universe, and thus threw doubt on the old assumptions, it brought also that Platonic theory and habit of mind which we have described: this turned into allegories many ancient beliefs which were recognized not to be literally true, and it could equally attribute a symbolic value to the old cosmic scheme, and to its poetic and moral associations.

Thus the old geo-centric and sphere-encircled universe always had a great hold on Milton's imagination, and he could not afford to give it up, even when he realized that science no longer supported it. For him it was linked to that vision of the glories of Heaven which was one of the permanent sources of his inspiration,[1] and in particular to the notion of the music of the spheres.[2] Milton's special feeling for this Pythagorean and Platonic conception, together with his recognition that it was more poetic than factual, is best illustrated by a passage in one of the Latin exercises of his university years, the second of his *Prolusions*, 'On the Harmony of the Spheres'. He begins by arguing that Pythagoras could not have intended the theory to be taken literally, and continues:

Certainly, if he taught a harmony of the spheres, and a revolution of the heavens to that sweet music, he wished to symbolize in a wise way the intimate relations of the spheres and their even revolution forever in accordance with the law of destiny. In this he seems to have followed the example of the poets—or, what is almost the same thing, of the divine oracles—by which no sacred and arcane mystery is ever revealed to vulgar ears without being somehow wrapped up and veiled. The greatest of Mother Nature's interpreters, Plato, has followed him, for he has told us that certain sirens have their respective seats on every one of the heavenly spheres and hold both gods and men fast bound by the wonder of their utterly harmonious song. And that universal interaction of all things, that lovely concord among them, which Pythagoras poetically symbolized as harmony, was splendidly and aptly represented by Homer's figure of the golden chain which Jove suspended from heaven. . . .

Hence arose also that primeval story that the Muses dance day and night before Jove's altar; and hence comes that ancient attribution of skill with the lyre to Apollo. . . .

What though no one on earth has ever heard that symphony of the stars? . . . Let us blame our own impotent ears, which cannot catch the songs or are unworthy to hear such sweet strains.

[1] See *On Time* and *At a Solemn Music*, n.
[2] See Nativity Ode, ll. 101-3 n.

... For how can we, whose spirits ... are warped earthward, and are defective in every heavenly element, be sensitive to that celestial sound? If our hearts were as pure, as chaste, as snowy as Pythagoras' was, our ears would resound and be filled with that supremely lovely music of the wheeling stars. Then indeed all things would seem to return to the age of gold. Then we should be immune to pain, and we should enjoy the blessing of a peace that the gods themselves might envy.[1]

[1] John Milton, *Complete Poems and Major Prose*, ed. Merritt Y. Hughes (New York, 1957), pp. 603-4.

The Chronology of Milton's Life

1608 Born in Bread Street, Cheapside, London, 9 December. 'His father John Milton, an honest, worthy, and substantial citizen of London, by profession a scrivener' (Edward Phillips).

1620 Entered St. Paul's School.

1625 Matriculated at Christ's College, Cambridge, 12 February. Charles I became King, March.

1629 Took B.A. degree, March.
     Wrote *On the Morning of Christ's Nativity*, December.

1632 Took M.A. degree, July.
     Settled at Horton in Buckinghamshire, where he lived until April 1638. *Sonnet II*, December.

1633 Laud became Archbishop of Canterbury.

1634 *Comus* performed at Ludlow Castle, 29 September.

1637 *Lycidas*, November. *Comus* published anonymously by Henry Lawes.

1638–9 *Lycidas* printed under signature J. M., in *Justa Edouardo King*, Cambridge. Milton left for continental tour in April 1638. Visited Paris, Florence, Rome, Naples, Venice, Geneva. Returned to England in August 1639.

1639 War with Scotland (First Bishops' War), March.

1639–40 Settled in London.

1640 Took as pupils his nephews, John and Edward Phillips. Short Parliament. Second Bishops' War, August.
     Long Parliament met, November. Laud and Strafford impeached.

1641–2 Began pamphleteering for the abolition of episcopacy. Five tracts on the question: *Of Reformation in England*; *Of Prelatical Episcopacy*; *Animadversions upon the Remonstrant's Defence*; *The Reason of Church Government*; *Apology for Smectymnuus*.

1641 Execution of Strafford. Irish Rebellion.

1642 Married Mary Powell in May or June. She was the daughter of Richard Powell of Forest Hill, near Shotover, in Oxfordshire; and returned to her family, who were Royalists, after about a month of married life in London.

Preparations for civil war. Battle of Edgehill, 23 October. *Sonnet III*, November.

1643–5 Published four divorce tracts: *The Doctrine and Discipline of Divorce*; *The Judgement of Martin Bucer Concerning Divorce*; *Tetrachordon*; *Colasterion*.

1644 Prose tracts: *Of Education* and *Areopagitica* ('For the Liberty of Unlicenc'd Printing').

Battles of Marston Moor and Newbury.

1645 Victory of Cromwell's New Model army at the Battle of Naseby, June.

Milton and his wife reconciled, July or August.

Moved to a house in Barbican.

1645–6 *Poems by Mr John Milton* published.

1646 First child, Anne, born 29 July.

Powell family took refuge with the Miltons for a time.

1647 Milton's father died, March.

1648 Second child, Mary, born 25 October.

Sonnet XI.

1649 Execution of Charles I, January.

Milton wrote *The Tenure of Kings and Magistrates*, February; and was appointed Secretary for Foreign Tongues to the Council of State in March.

Eikonoklastes, October.

1651 Third child, John, born 16 March, died in infancy.

Defensio pro Populo Anglicano, February.

Granted assistance in office, owing to failing sight.

1652 Total blindness.

Fourth child, Deborah, born 2 May; Mary Powell died, 5 May.

1653 Cromwell became Lord Protector.

1654 *Defensio Secunda*.

1655 *Defensio pro Se*. *Sonnets XIV, XVIII*.

1656 Married Katherine Woodcock, November.

1657 Daughter born, October.

1658 Wife and infant daughter died, February and March.

Death of Cromwell, September.

1659 Two tracts on behalf of religious freedom and against church establishment, February and August.

Abdication of Richard Cromwell, May.

1660 *The Ready and Easy Way to Establish a Free Commonwealth*, March.

Dismissed from office. Went into hiding in a friend's house in Bartholomew Close.

Restoration of Charles II, May. Act of Oblivion. Milton was exempted from prosecution through the influence of his friend Andrew Marvell and other Members of Parliament.

1663 Married Elizabeth Minshull, February.

Moved to a house in Artillery Walk, Bunhill Fields.

1667 *Paradise Lost* published.

1671 *Paradise Regain'd* and *Samson Agonistes* published.

1673 Second and enlarged edition of *Poems*.

Published his last prose tract, a plea for mutual tolerance among Protestants: *Of True Religion, Heresy, Schism, Toleration; and What Best Means may be used against the Growth of Popery*.

1674 Second edition of *Paradise Lost*.

Milton died, 8 November; buried in St. Giles', Cripplegate.

Rape is foundational.

Orgel made Cennus the
center of the play

Asked us to see the play from
Cennus's point of view —

We do when we read his
speeches.